FROM AUTHOR "SIXX" KING

GIVING LO♥E
A CHANCE

The secrets to Men, Women & Relationships

Published by:
New Wall Street Publishing
63 Wall Street, Suite 1710
New York, NY 10014

www.givingloveachance.com

Astrology Data: Martine Sexual Astrology,
A Sign by Sign Guide to Your Sensual Stars

Designed by:
Chase Preston, Robert Michael & Shawna A. Grundy

Printed in the United States of America

ISBN: 978-0-557-62677-9

GIVING LOVE A CHANCE

The secrets to Men, Women & Relationships

Acknowledgements

First I would like to thank my parents Christian & Abiona Adadevoh. I think that I take the best traits of both you to become the man that I am today mom you've always allowed me to dream big and do even bigger "Thoughts are things" Without you there would be no me simply put I love you eternally! Dad your advice has been priceless and your prayers are heard loud and clear by God almighty!

I thank my son, Najee, for choosing me to be your father. You're the very heartbeat of my life and I'm so proud of you. "Make it happen, Make it count" is the motto!

I would like to thank my team Jhonn Puente, Taleeb Starkes, Alisa Payne, Richard Washington, Charles Phillips, Dyana Williams.

I would like to thank my editor Catherine Staples as well as my designers Chase Phillips & Robert Michaels for their diligent work in giving this project the ultimate look of happiness & love.

When I think of courage, survivor, & constant professional there are only two words that come to my mind "Shawna Grundy". Your work is immeasurable.

I would like to thank my Essence.com family, Emil Wilbekin & Lesely Pickney for allowing me such a broad spectrum to express myself I salute you with the greatest gratitude.

In memory of my Uncle Roland aka Abugunde, your life long love for me and guidance are the essential things I have passed on to my son. I can never thank you enough, my grandmother Madam Edith Afiwor Fiawoo Adadevoh (Ewotsige) you're highly favored and truly blessed. I miss you and love you. Joan Williams-Balfe, thank you for believing in this project from the inception. You're loved and missed by me.

I would like to thank all of my brothers and sisters who make me proud in every way long live the Adadevoh family

Preface

I was 29 years old and quickly approaching thirty. For many men, this is the prime time to party, enjoy the single life and indulge in as much sexual activity as possible. These men plan to "settle down" sometime between their late thirties and early forties, so it seems logical to them that they should sow their wild oats—as many oats as possible—until they settle down. To me that logic was debatable. My grandmother always expressed to me that the older a tree gets, the harder it is to bend with each blowing wind. That proverb made more sense to me than the logic of my cohort, especially because it was coming from a woman who has been happily married for 60 years!

I believe that the older one gets, the more difficult it becomes to compromise in a relationship, especially when the two people are not growing together. I have been in and out of relationships since I was 15 years old. Even at that young age, I instinctively knew what a good woman was. But I always chose women who were challenges. Although my heart sensed that these particular women were disagreeable to my well being, the hunter/conqueror in me would still push me to aggressively pursue any woman that posed a challenge. I knew that this mindset would plague me for the rest of my dating life if I didn't take corrective action. I eventually discovered that I wasn't alone in practicing these counterproductive habits. It was a pleasant surprise to learn that I wasn't alone. Many of my friends were guilty of the same actions.

So I decided to do some research. I found 20 men and 20 women who had never met each other, and I invited them to my place to engage in some real and honest dialogue about the opposite sex. I asked everyone to leave their representatives at home and prepare to be truthful, candid and revealing about their own gender. These continued discussions, which were aimed at unlocking the secrets of the opposite sex's mindset, would prove to be life changing for me and for everyone who attended those gatherings.

It seems to me that most people fear relationships that are naturally good for/to them. Oftentimes, they shun that agreeable relationship and gravitate toward the opposite one. To them, success is determined by their repeated attempts at defying nature to make bad relationships work. I knew this all too well, so I decided to make myself a promise. The promise was that I would remove myself from this vicious cycle and embrace what's good for me. I would learn to fear eminent failure not eminent success. In addition, I would look within myself to transform the bad into good, and the good into greatness! My grandmother always said, "When you point the finger at someone, four of those fingers are pointing back at you!" I interpreted that to mean that taking self-inventory is a necessary first-step toward positive growth. For the first time since I was fifteen, I wasn't in a relationship. Instead, I was on a journey to find the answers to the questions that we all have about love. I was giving love a break by discovering what love really was.

Table of Contents

My Personal Trials and Tribulations

While writing this book I was going through a very difficult time in my life. It seemed as though for every step that I took to improve my life, certain circumstances turned those steps of improvement counter-productive. I had just emerged from a relationship that I truly intended to grow into something forever lasting, but in life everything you potentially plan for does not always come to fruition. Being truly not involved or in a relationship was a defining moment for me as a man. I had reached a crossroad in my life where I could give in to pessimism, bitterness, and anger or I could embrace optimism, love and hope. I could throw myself a bitter party, be scorned as a man and forego everything my mother taught me about being a good man, or I could make the harder choice and continue to move forward. I chose to take the path of self-inventory and self-deprecation. I learned that when you bounce from one relationship to the next, you never really get a chance to assess your accountability. To this day, just admitting those faults still leaves me with a sense of vulnerability that no one wants to reveal. As an individual it's easier to pass the blame than it is to take an inventory of your faults and bad decisions. I've come to learn that when you're truly honest with yourself you can truly be honest with others, and that mistakes in life recognized and corrected shows growth in a person who chooses to grow. Over the course of the four years that it took me to write this book, my dating life was a book in itself. The dating climate had changed dramatically, and I found that most women had adopted the ways of bad men. The rules for dating had totally changed. For the first few months, it seemed that every woman I met was just as dishonest as the next. I didn't have to look for this dishonesty to find it because what you do in the dark shall come to the light. If it wasn't dishonesty, it was mental drama or a selfishness so thick you could cut it with a knife. The dating climate was so crazy that it had the potential to make me a very frustrated person, which plagues a lot of people—men and women—who are just searching for simplicity. I decided to stop expecting so much from one person and start expecting much more from myself. I pledged not to try to upgrade the women I dated but to upgrade myself to a different caliber of women to date. I think for many people it's easier to be who you are then to be who you're not. Please don't expect to find your qualities instilled in everyone you meet. It's unrealistic. Having more things in common then not proves to be a more successful path for people who are looking to build a lasting relationship. When I started dating again, there were a few questions I would ask women. What is good about you and what is bad about you? That simple question told me a lot about the woman and her ability to be totally honest with herself. The majority of the women who responded to the question had nothing bad to say about themselves, and those who admitted anything bad about themselves usually had answers that were very self-serving such as, "I'm too nice," etc. I now understood that self-honesty was very difficult, not only for me, but for others as well, and to correct that common flaw that we may all suffer from I would need to dig deep and hard to change. The first step for me was to learn self-discipline and to focus better on the task at hand, which was to work on my many issues such as being a better listener, not taking a small problem and snowballing it into a bigger one because I didn't have all the answers right away, understanding that I was a veteran in the relationship department and that no situation was too foreign to me and that my experience, if I practiced it, wouldn't allow me to control the situation better. I had to learn not to let my low tolerance for nonsense affect my ability to be understanding and diplomatic. I learned that people tell you who they are, and it's up to you to listen and not let your lust cloud your ability to make good decisions. I encourage everyone who is dating again to stop looking for a relationship and start focusing on the type of relationship that's good for you. I encourage you to let someone's actions replace his or her words. It's always good to hear that you're loved, but it's better to be shown that you're loved. I come from a family where marriage is taken seriously and not just as a novelty or an accessory.

INTRODUCTION

The Focus Group

When I first started the focus group, I was coming out of many failed relationships, and I really wanted to obtain a wealth of information about women that I didn't have in my arsenal as a smooth, problem-solving man. I had it all planned out. I would invite over a few women and men for some of my famous cooking and drink mixing abilities, and when the time was right, like a mission impossible agent on assignment to save the world, I would descend on the bevy of intelligent women that were now intoxicated and ripe, and I would cleverly pick their brains to learn what women really want. I would then be able to apply that valuable information to my next relationship, and I would become the ultimate success rather than the ultimate failure. My selfish motives came to a screeching halt when the sessions turned into something much greater than I expected—a life changing and defining moment for me as a man. Everything that I thought I knew about women I didn't know and vice versa. I was stunned when I found out, as did most men who attended the group, how self-medicated we all were because as men, we don't ask for directions when we are lost in a car or in our dating life; we just continue on the road to lost and confused until ultimately we run out of gas or eventually find our way by some stroke of luck. The sessions also proved how far off men and women really were in terms of communication. Each person came to the sessions with his or her relationship issues. As we began to engage in deep conversations about what successful relationships consist of, we discovered that we all had experienced some of the same pitfalls of failed relationships and that through really revealing the coded language of the opposite sex, we would unlock the secrets of Men, Women, and Relationships. Our initial sessions started out with the fundamental differences between men and women such as "Why do men leave the toilet seat up?" as well as "Why do women want to have a heart to heart talk during the Super Bowl? Please just pass the remote and the nachos and be quiet." When those discussions finally died down and we could really get to the core of why and what makes the opposite sex tick, we all discovered that we were not as different as we thought and that if approached by the right methods we could enter into a relationship that worked for us as opposed to one that worked against us. One by one, I witnessed the men and women in the focus group go on to enter successful, lasting relationships and marriages using what they had learned to build and maintain their newly found unions. Some had to come back and get a refresher course on the secrets to success, but like anything of quality, you will always need a tune up here and there to keep a consistent pace on the road to success.

Chapter 1

Facing the Reflection of Who You Are

Balance

The first topic I opened the group discussions with was that of balance and how it is achieved throughout relationships. This issue plagued each and every attendee in some form or another. Achieving balance was something that most attendees wanted to master, both professionally and personally. Being off balance is not as uncommon as one would think. We've all heard that old saying, "Never judge a book by its cover." The relationships we think are well balanced are sometimes the most unbalanced of them all, but these same relationships can become balanced when we approach them with creativity. Sometimes the simplest changes can stimulate the kind of balance that we all need to achieve success.

I, for one, was a very unbalanced individual when it came to my career and my personal life. There were no grey areas in my life. I lacked the balance I needed to work and live in a healthy way to spread my work ethic evenly and successfully. Attempting a balancing act was as challenging for me as the first attempts to place a man on the moon. At one point, my career was on the rise, and then came what I call, "Love and Molasses." I fell in love and immediately, my career almost came to a standstill. What had seemed like a fast rise to mogul status was suddenly stalled as I became more concerned with love than with the task at hand, which was becoming a billionaire before I was thirty. I now believe that for a driven person such as myself, a balanced relationship is best achieved with someone who is similarly driven—someone can appreciate quality over quantity. One mistake that most of us make is we are not honest about what we require to maintain ourselves and to be fulfilled in our relationships. Some plants, such as a cactus, require little water to stay alive, and some, such as roses, require a great deal of everything to prevent wilting. We all learned from this discussion that the key to balance is an unselfish work ethic towards your partner; want for your sister what you would want for yourself, and vice versa. However, self-truth has to play a key part. It is essential that we be upfront and honest about our personal requirements. What do you need to maintain who you are? Are you a cactus or a rose?

Adding to your Character

I think that the oldest misconception we all have is that we can get something for nothing. If you want to be successful in any relationship, you must work on your character. In the many discussions we had, folks said that they often miss out on the chance to develop beneficial traits because they are afraid to challenge themselves. I am a true believer that what is added to your character becomes much more of a natural act instead of a choir, because as we all understand that choirs become repetitive and soon unbearable to complete, the more positive traits you add to your character the greater chance you have of being consistent in a positive way not only to yourself but to your potential mate.

Want More for Yourself

Some people get so frustrated with the opposite sex that they devalue their own self worth. You cannot measure your own value by the actions of others in this world. If you do, then you will always come up short. In my many discussions about men and women, I have found that some women and men have arrived at a destination in their dating lives where they only see their relationships as having materialistic value—bills paid, clothes, sex, dinner, trips, etc. Those who primarily value material things will in general become of no more value than the things they seek from the other person. Truly listen to people when conversing with them and you will learn a lot more about that person's true intentions than you will ever learn over a longer period of time if you are not listening to what's coming out of their mouths. There some people who arrange their lives so that they only eat side dishes and never the main course. You can never build anything with these people because they require little and produce little. When you want more for yourself, you are able to contribute more to others who are willing and worthy of your contributions.

When you only go for the crumbs of a cake you will never taste the richness of the cake in its entirety.
~Abgazd Hovedada 1972–

The Definition of You

Too many times we define ourselves by others' actions. One of the greatest leaders of our time, Martin Luther King, turned the other cheek, not to be smacked again, but to look into a new direction and take a new course of action. Turning one's cheek in this way preserves the individual and reduces the negative energy from an already volatile situation. When we take a new direction that is satisfying to our hearts and souls, we embark on new and productive ground sometimes as couples and sometimes alone!

In order to grow and flourish in any situation, you must approach life without limitations. The definition of who you are should never be summed up in a single sentence or paragraph. There should be many dimensions in that definition as you continuously create different facets of your life and legacy.

Growth demands a temporary surrender of security.
~Gail Sheehy, 1937–

We All Fall Down

The first time you were hurt in a relationship was probably the most tragic thing you had ever experienced in life. But we all fall down. It's when you don't get up from that experience and continue to soak in the pain of the past that you kill your own intimate growth as a person. It's always easier said than done because words spoken fill our space faster than our mental progression will allow. However, it is those spoken words that you must use to navigate through the maze of webs you weave to protect yourself from future disappointments. How can someone else truly see who you are if the best part of yourself is hidden?

Everyone is willing to learn from an unpleasant experience—if only the damage of the first lesson could be repaired.
~Georg Christoph Lichtenberg, 1742–1799

Finding Your Comfort Zone

So many of us have a hard time finding our comfort zone after ending a relationship because of the constant social pressure about not being alone. When you find your comfort zone and relax, your focus is better. Have you ever looked so hard for something that you looked right past it? When you finally said, "OK, let me relax and not make this a microwave situation—instant gratification," did what you were looking for appear right before you? When you find a comfort zone within yourself, you will no longer have to look for anything; it will appear right before your eyes. You have to be able to say, "I'm ok with myself." Being OK with yourself will draw others to you.

Individualism is like innocence: There must be something
unconscious about it.
~Louis Kronenberger, 1904–1980

Chapter 2

Take a Look at You Now

You Know Who You Are

S ome people can "cast" you according to their own desires and intentions, but you are never a mere reflection of what anyone else wants. Never let anyone cast you in role that is not yours. Know who you really are as opposed to what other people want you to be. Sometimes, trying to explain that you are not the person someone else wants you to be only wastes precious life, air, and time. Your light and ambitions as an individual are not up for dissection as if you were a cadaver in a laboratory.

Never explain. Your friends do not need it and your enemies will
never believe it anyway.
~Elbert Hubbard, 1856–1915

You Know the Answer

We all know the answer to what needs to be done throughout our relationships. If the relationship is good, we know what work is needed to keep it good. If it is bad, we also know when to throw in the towel. As a people, we should not let our endurance for life, work, or religion make us a martyr for foolishness.

Advice is what we look for when we already know the answer but
wish we didn't.
~Erica Jong, 1942–

I Am Not You

So often we get upset because other people don't approach or handle situations as we would. People are always going to be different; that is what makes the world go around and what keeps the balance of life interesting and challenging. We are all guilty of hoping what we consider our great qualities will be adopted by our partners. We want them to share our own rules of thumb about how to handle things and how to be. Although it is often beneficial for couples to adopt each other's ideas, there will always be differences, and you only have two choices—deal with them, or don't.

Be not angry that you cannot make others as you wish them to be,
since you cannot make yourself as you wish to be.
~Thomas `a Kempis, 1380–1471

Man in the Mirror

When I ask people what they look for in the perfect individual to have a relationship with, most of them describe everything they are not, and everything they hope to become. Some people claim that they attract a certain type of individual and that they are constantly searching to find their other half. A search like this can seem like a never-ending battle, but if you change direction, you are certainly guaranteed new scenery. Fulfillment starts within you; you must provide what you need to complete yourself.

A loving person lives in a loving world. A hostile person lives in a hostile world: everyone you meet is your mirror.
~Ken Keyes, Jr. 1921–1995

Everyone is Not You

Some of us always assume that the way we approach or handle certain things in life is universal. If others approach things differently, we really think they should adopt our approach. Unfortunately, that rarely happens. In certain scenarios, you may approach something in a way that seems right to a majority of others. You may have clear expectations about the way you should be treated in your time of need based on how you treat others in their time of need. You are who you are, and that's what makes you different from all human beings on this earth. Dealing with someone who is like-minded always makes relationships run more smoothly because what you feel is sensible will never be an issue.

As I know more of mankind I expect less of them, and am ready now to call a man a good man upon easier terms than I was formerly.
~Dr. Samuel Johnson, 1709–1784

Me, Myself and I

Self-preservation is the first rule of nature, and if we do not take the time and effort to make sure that our own well-being is intact, then what we have to offer to other people will come up short every time. Some people give so much of themselves throughout life that they have no energy to refuel themselves to normal capacity. It is OK to say, "I need a break and a chance to get back some of what I give on a day-to-day basis so that I can be the best person I can be in this relationship."

We have to serve ourselves
many years before we gain our own confidence.
~Henry S. Haskins, 1878–1957

Chapter 3

Great Wine Equals Great Reflection Time

A Letter to Love

It's been a while since I've experienced the wonderful fascists that you have to offer when you're in my company. So many different things have occurred in my life since we've parted ways, but I look forward to your return. When we first went our separate ways, I vowed never to deal with you again. I was angry and hurt. But I soon realized it wasn't you that I dreaded, it was your absence that I dreaded. When we were together I felt like I could conquer the world—my passion for doing things became ten times greater. The smile that you kept on my face was priceless, and the enthusiasm that flowed throughout my soul was a miracle in itself. I ask myself on a daily basis where I went wrong, and then as I take the time out to stop and listen, I hear your soft whispers that say you're still here, silently residing in my heart, waiting for that phone call to come back into my life. As I screen out the hopefuls or the maybes to invite them over for your grand entrance, I patiently enjoy our time alone, that was something I had to learn to do. I always felt that in order to fully enjoy you, I had to wait for someone else to tell me that you were visiting them as well and that it took two versions of you to equal one, when in fact, that's not the case. I've learned that you have many hearts that you call home, and I'm honored that you still reside in mine.

There are three important steps in a man's life: birth, marriage, and death...but necessarily not in that order.
~John M. Shanahan, 1939–

If You're So Good, Why Aren't You Married Yet?

I didn't become the man I am today without trial and error. Throughout my growing process, there have been some casualties along my path. As I have grown, some of life's lessons have come with pain, both given and received. I am not a malicious man, and I pray that no one has suffered an eternity of pain throughout my process of finding my way. I've never been a perfect man, but I am a man with a conscience and conviction of my own actions. I strive to be a man who takes his own self-inventory and corrects those things that I know to be wrong and tries to make them right. It's not easy looking at the things that are bad about yourself with no one to blame but yourself. I know in my heart when you only reflect on what is good about yourself and don't face the negative, you can't grow. My quest has taken me on quite a journey, and I have grown as a man more than I ever imagined I could. I can honestly and proudly say that I am a better man today than I was yesterday.

They say men are molded out of faults, and for the most, become much more the better for being a little bad.
~William Shakespeare, 1564–1616

Almost to the Altar

I once stared true love directly in the face. I had never in my life had someone love me as unconditionally as she did. Our days were filled with a lot of laughter and good times. She embraced family the way I did, and the Sunday dinners at her mother's house were like something out of a movie; everyone was a character, and you could feel the love throughout. She was beautiful, outside and inside and I thought I was truly the luckiest man in the world. Then the unthinkable happened. A series of unfortunate events happen to me, and these events affected me physically, financially, spiritually and emotionally. I felt like I was a fraction of the man that I needed to be in order to maintain the relationship. When she looked at me, she recognized a king in need of his queen. When I looked at myself, I saw failure. Pride was my new crown, and instead of communicating, I cut the lines of communication off instantly, taking her choice away to be the real woman she was and hang in there with me through the darkest days of my life. As I strayed, she prayed, and through each of her prayers I was blessed. But pride was still my crown, and the thought of someone loving me so unconditionally was my prejudice. She had given her heart to me, and I handed it back to her with pain and confusion. This caused an eternal emotional roller coaster for her. We separated, but not fully. I was blind to the reality of our situation until one day, sitting in front of her; I noticed that she was wearing an engagement ring. For the first time, it became real to me that I was losing this woman who loved me so much. I tried to tell her how I felt, but even then, my attempt to make her understand how I really felt fell short. The prideful part of me wouldn't let the words from my heart reach my mouth. She said that she had prayed for a good man to come into her life and that her prayers had been answered. I knew right then that God had truly spoken for one of his angels. Her prayers saved my life, her love became my strength, and not a day has gone by that I haven't felt her absence greatly. My only solace is that I am one of the few people who have shared true love and lost true love only to have it reside in my heart for eternity.

True love is like ghosts,
which everybody talks about and few have seen.
~Francois, Duc de La Rochefoucauld, 1613–1680

The Reality of Losing Love...

As my relationship ended I first felt all of these different emotions: anger, fear, hurt, betrayal and disappointment. The first few months were hell because some things other than the break-up were going on in my life, and the one person I had turned to for support wasn't there. The reality of losing love and my best friend hit me like a ton of bricks! One morning as I was riding the train from Harlem and bobbing my head to my ipod, a woman sat next to me and the fragrance that she was wearing reminded me of my ex. I immediately started thinking about her and our relationship and where we went wrong. As a small smile appeared on my face, I started reminiscing about some of the crazy but good times we had together, and in that instant a rush of emotions overwhelmed me, and I just broke down crying right there on the train. The harder I tried to get my composure, the more the tears flooded down my face. I am not a man who cries easily, but for me it wasn't just this particular relationship that I wept for, but a culmination of failed attempts at love followed by years of self-medication, self-diagnosis, and a continued behavior of moving on without healing first. I learned that when you're in the heat of battle, the wounds you receive don't affect you right away because of all of the adrenaline and emotions that you are experiencing during the battle. However, when all is calm and you mentally realize everything that has taken place, the wounds you received start to ache. I was aching, but I knew that these feelings and emotions were a part of my healing process, and that I had to let it take its course. During that process, the hardest thing for me to do was to forgive my ex for the pain I felt. I wanted her to hurt just like I was hurting, and the mere thought of ever forgiving her was far from my realm of reality. As time passed, my healing process moved into the more positive direction of forgiveness and true healing. True healing can only come when you truly forgive without any concern about who was right and who was wrong, and when you allow yourself to heal in that manner, no scars of your past battle will disable your heart from performing at full capacity.

Everyone is a prisoner of his own experiences. No one can eliminate prejudices—just recognize them.
~Edward Roscoe Murrow, 1908–1965

I Almost Lost Hope Until You Arrived

Thank you for being the reflection of everything that I believe in. Your words and grace are the soundtrack to my life. You are a constant reminder to me that my good work, love and dedication does exist outside of my own heart. I'm not naïve—I know that time will test us as it does all great things, for what is a boat if it never leaves the harbor and experiences the rough seas? Faith has always been one of the most difficult things for mankind to achieve because we are inclined to believe in what we can touch more than we believe in what we can envision. So when I express that my hope was almost lost, it's because my faith had been battered to the point of hopelessness. I've now learned that the closer I get to success, the harder the road will get. So, it thrills me to the point of perpetual elation that you've taken my hand and embarked on this journey of love, life and the pursuit of happiness.

Why am I so thankful for the things that God hasn't blessed me with as of yet?

- I'm so thankful that God hasn't blessed me with tons of money as of yet. Why? Because it shows me how to work with a little and give a lot.
- I'm so thankful that God hasn't blessed me with the anxiety of urgency as of yet. Why? It allows me to slow up and take in all of life's many dimensions, the good the bad and the ugly, in the hope that I will fully understand the balance of life.
- I'm so thankful that God hasn't blessed me with world fame as of yet. Why?
- It allows me more time to practice my speech and get it perfectly right in the hope that it will inspire the world to love more and give more.
- I'm so thankful that God hasn't blessed me with the promise

that I will live to see tomorrow. Why?

- It teaches me to enjoy each day in its entirety as if it were my last and to take more chances, love harder, stress less and really appreciate another gift called tomorrow.
- I'm so thankful that God hasn't blessed me with a wife as of yet. Why?
- It allows me more time to rehearse my wedding vows so that I can memorize them by heart and not nervously read them from a piece of paper, while taking the risk of them being washed away from my tears of joy.
- I'm so thankful that God hasn't blessed me with a set of eyes in the back of my head as of yet. Why?
- It teaches me that he's already watching my back and that when I practice my faith in him, there is no need for an extra set of eyes.
- I'm so thankful that God hasn't blessed me with all that I have asked of him as of yet. Why?
- It teaches me to remember that he already knows what I need and that he will give it to me as I need it and not a second later.

Chapter 4

Application of Advice

Advice for Women

One day while sitting at home, I was watching a television program on the Lion Kingdom, and it hit me that nature for every animal—and yes man is an animal—is the same across the board and that no amount of civilization will ever change that. I watched as the lioness prowled in the high grass to scope out her prey, knowing very well that the prey had to fulfill her needs as well as the needs of the rest of the pride. She needed to be careful not to pick prey that did not meet her requirements because if she did, all of the energy she used in the hunt would be in vain and it would sap her strength. When the fulfilling prey did come along, she wouldn't have the strength to move forward. Society may have you think that men are the hunters and women are the hunted, but fairy tales of a knight in shining armor whisking you off your feet are just that...fairy tales. Nature says that women are the hunters and men are the hunted. A woman will plan for a man what she wants for her future before he even knows what hit him. All men can do is to be good prey. I'm not trying to convey that all women should be aggressive when they meet a man. What I am saying is that you should rely on your instinct when choosing a man. What is fulfilling to you as a woman? Have you ever been in a relationship that you knew would not fulfill you as an individual—the fuel you need to keep being the best person you can be—but you told yourself something different? (Example: you give all that you have to that person physically, mentally, and emotionally. You go all out for the person, and in return he gives you a small gesture of appreciation. The gesture takes you totally by surprise and you're so happy, you say to yourself, "Yeah, this person will finally be the person I need." But you soon learn that his small gesture is as good as it gets, and he's not at all what you need. Does this sound familiar? Then, after wasting all that energy, when a guy comes along who does have everything you need—personality, finances, etc.—you don't have the strength to move forward. The greatest mistake in life is fearing that you will make a mistake. All mistakes are repeated until you master them, and you choose how many times to be the student and how many times to be the master.

Our names are labels,
plainly printed on the bottled essence of our past behavior.
~Logan Pearsall Smith, 1865–1946

Advice for Men

If you understand that the woman is the hunter and you are the prey, then you will understand that the most attractive prey always attracts the most hunters. Most men don't understand that women are just as sexual as men are—some even more so. The only difference is that women will never wear their full sexual intent on their sleeves as most men do. Men who exude confidence and patience, and who practice consistent execution usually succeed with women. A woman knows from the very first conversation she has with you if you're a potential sexual mate. Your initial conversation will determine what category she places you in. It has been proven that an honest man will progress further in the type of relationship he chooses to have than a dishonest man. Most women can handle the truth, but when you deceive them by trying to manipulate their perception of how the relationship will progress, then all bets are off. And remember, hell hath no fury like a woman scorned.

> *That's the nature of women, not to love when we love them,*
> *and to love when we love them not.*
> ~Miguel de Cervantes, 1547–1616

> *I present myself to you in a form suitable to the relationship*
> *I wish to achieve with you.*
> ~Luigi Pirandello, 1867–1936

Advice for Women

Getting the best out of any man is a simple thing to do, "stroke the hell out of his ego". As men, we love praise for what we do, and we can get discouraged very quickly when don't get that praise. When you let a man know that you appreciate him and his efforts toward pleasing you, he will be more likely to take your constructive criticism about things that may have fallen short of your expectations as constructive and rather than destructive. As a woman you have to remember that man may be the head, but woman is the neck, and the neck controls the head. Once you've mastered the technique of stroking, you can get a man to do almost anything (i.e., talk with you more, help with household chores, and ask for directions when lost).

> *Anybody who believes that the way to a man's heart*
> *is through his stomach flunked geography.*
> ~Robert Byrne 1939–

Advice for Men

Women love what they haven't totally conquered. Stay one step ahead of her at all times. Most men are so predictable and routine that they have a hard time keeping women interested. This is the leading reason that good women fall for bad boys. The bad boy's unpredictability and sense of adventure is an instant attraction to an already curious species. A woman might like a bad boy for the adventure but he may not necessarily be the person she wants to share a mortgage with later. Women look for a combination of stability and adventure. Most men opt out of showing and sharing their drive and passions with their mates, never fully understanding that their passions are what attracted their mates to them in the first place. Always keep a women guessing, and never be afraid to change up and add some spontaneity to your personality. To be a hit with women, it's not enough to just come up with great ideas. To have the most success with women, you need to consistently execute your great ideas.

Woman inspires us to do great things,
and Men prevent themselves from achieving them.
~Alexandre Dumas

Advice for Women

Why do men cheat? Some men are as faithful as their options allow them to be; other men simply cheat out of curiosity. Do all men cheat? No! Most men think of sex as a physical act, whereas women generally associate sex with emotions. How a man handles temptation is essential to him staying monogamous in his relationship. Most men do not think about loyalty to their mates in the same way that they think about loyalty to their male friends. Additionally, most men won't lie to their male friends or do something to outright hurt or betray them, but those same men often hurt or betray their mates by cheating on them. Remember, men typically don't have emotional attachments when having "cheating" sex with another woman. They can love their wives to death and still have sex with someone else, then go home to a loving wife with no change in their feelings toward her. Once you've established the same loyalty with a man that he has with his male friends, he will most likely never commit infidelity because of the loyalty factor towards you. Have you noticed that a man is less forgiving when he catches a woman cheating? That's because in his mind he's saying, "You actually like this guy!" Loyalty to a man is what emotional connections are to a woman.

As a rule the person found out in a betrayal of love holds, all the same, the superior position of the two.
It is the betrayed one who is humiliated.
~Ada Leverson, 1865–1936

Advice for Men

Why do women cheat? A woman cheats for many different reasons, but her main reason is that her relationship does not fulfill her emotionally. When a woman has experienced emotional deficiency in a relationship, she will eventually fill that void with someone who is capable of giving her what she needs. Unlike a man, her departure will be subtle and well thought-out. As she moves to emotionally detach herself from her unsatisfactory situation, her mate may not even notice. Most men neglect to pay attention to women's subtle changes in routine and behavior thus allowing for a high rate of success in women's infidelity. Some women think about infidelity the way men do, but for the average woman, emotional gratification is a must. Her need to be thoroughly listened to is strong. Although you may not be capable of fixing her immediate problem, you will show her that you care by listening and letting her vent. Most men think that women want them to fix every frustrating situation, but that theory is very far from the truth.

The man who lends an ear will prevail in the end.

All men are tempted. There is no man that lives that can't be broken down, provided it is the right temptation, put in the right spot.
~Henry Ward Beecher 1813–1887

Advice for Women

Finding a good man is not like looking for a needle in a haystack. Just as everyone has fifteen minutes of fame, every woman will have a good man enter her life. You will have many opportunities to choose a man as good and not-so-good men enter and depart from your life. It's up to you to decide when you're ready to choose a man and whether you will choose Mr. Right, Mr. Right Now or Mr. Wrong. Most women and men are fully aware when a relationship is good for them, but it's our curiosity and greed as human beings that will not always allow us to be satisfied, thus giving credence to the old saying "what's good for you is seldom what you're attracted too". I'm not suggesting that you should deny your passions when choosing a mate, but understand that you're not going to get everything you want from one individual. It's impossible and unrealistic. However, you should always get from a man what you need to be the best person you can be. If you pick from the same tree each time, don't expect to get a different fruit. I call this the Eve syndrome. Please shake it. At some point, you have to be totally honest with yourself and say, "This is who I am, and this is what I need to always keep my best foot forward." Stop challenging yourself to a battle that can never be won, and stop catering to your maternal instinct, thinking that you can teach a man to become what you need. Remember, some people can be with you but not for you.

Never have a companion that casts you in the shade.
~Baltasar Gracian, 1601–1691

Advice for Men

Most men are not in to keep a woman intrigued. When dealing with a woman, you must learn to have confidence in what's interesting about yourself. Women love a man who has a precise idea about what to do and who exudes a confidence of leadership, a take-control type of man, not a controlling man. There is a big difference between the two. A take-control type of man can handle any situation, which benefits himself as well as his mate, whereas a controlling man has no clue, and doesn't care about what he's doing, just as long as he is in control. You are your own best advertisement. When a man takes the time to invest in himself without being selfish, he will attract women who are intrigued with his confidence to lead—remember, they are the hunters. Women soak up everything you say, your sense of fashion, how you smell, etc. Never let a woman totally figure you out. I'm not saying give her a fake name and have a secret family who she only meets at your funeral, but keep her guessing all the time and she will always want more. Once a woman thinks she has you lock, stock and barrel, there is no need for her to stay on her "A" game.

Men who cherish for women the highest respect
are seldom popular with them.
~Anonymous

Advice for Women

Men are taught from the time they are a born to tuck the emotions and take it like a man, so our capabilities of sharing how we truly feel are usually stunted from early growth. No woman would really want a man who is too sensitive; however, most women do appreciate a man who caters to their sensitivity issues. Men are more vulnerable emotionally than most women would imagine, and this usually causes men to be very unforgiving when they are hurt or betrayed. When a man experiences being hurt, his emotional inadequacy doesn't allow him to easily forgive or continue to choose optimism when dealing with a woman. A man will only grant the coveted access to his heart to a woman who is able to practice patience. He needs to trust that you won't use the very subjects he shares with you as ammunition or emotional retribution in a fight. Women who use persistence and aggravation will always fail at gaining a man's trust. In general, men bond and open up better in a casual atmosphere that is not so focused on feelings and emotions. The common mistake women make is trying to connect with a man as they do with other women. Again, men are not as well-equipped to handle their emotions as you are. They can't just experience intense emotion as a cathartic experience and then easily transition to cocktails and shopping. Men connect in ways that are far different from the way women connect. If you practice your approach with this in mind, you will in turn receive what you need to connect on a much higher level than you would otherwise.

A wife is to thank God her husband hath faults…
A husband without faults is a dangerous observer.
~George Savile, Marquess de Halifax, 1633–1691

Advice for Men

Most men approach sex with women as if they are the greatest lover of all time, never once feeling that they have to change anything when it comes to intimacy. A smart man will quickly understand that what works for one woman doesn't always work for the next. A man's ego and arrogance usually thwarts his efforts of attaining the title, "greatest lover of all time." The reason that most women are better lovers than men is that they never stop seeking knowledge of how to be a better lover, and more important, how to be a different lover. Most men have not changed their style of sex since they started having sex. Women have sex parties to keep up with the latest craze in the bedroom, while men bask in the glory of old victories. It does you all the good in the world to explore more about intimacy with women; you'll realize that you don't have a clue about some things you thought you knew. It's good to explore and research how to be a better lover, and most important, how to be an unselfish lover because women know the difference. Always be willing to learn from a woman what she likes and wants during intimacy, for it will show her your attentiveness to not only receive pleasure but also to give pleasure as well.

The things we know best are the things we haven't been taught.
~Luc de Clapiers de Vauvenargues, 1715–1747

Advice For Women

Most women take past experiences as guides for entering new relationships. They make rules and regulations of what is to be and what is not to be. Some women claim that this their way of protecting themselves from repeating the bad things that happened in their past relationships. The truth of the matter is that for most men, navigating through your fortress of protection can be an instant turn-off, and in reality, when you cast such a wide net, the good ones get caught up as well. The men who will do the most damage will wait out your defense timeline only to do what you have so heavily guarded against. Most men with good intentions have not the time nor the patience to pay for the previous damage. I'm not advising you not to learn from your past mistakes, but I am saying that past bad experiences should not be used as a method of defense but rather as a tool to help you make better choices. Remember, when you pick from the same tree you will get the same fruit.

Vows begin when hope dies.
~Leonardo da Vinci, 1452–1519

Advice For Women

When a man meets a good woman who has her life on point and knows what she wants, he will approach her using one of three different avenues, depending on where he is in his life. He will either:

> ➤ Drag you through his ups and downs until he gets his act together
> ➤ Become the most indecisive individual you have ever met as he ponders whether he wants to be in a relationship or not, or
> ➤ Take you very seriously, and start to clear the way for a monogamous relationship with you.

If a man is practicing one of the first two scenarios, you should cut your losses, and move forward for the sake of your own peace of mind and sanity. Women make the mistake of envisioning the possibilities of what a relationship could be instead of seeing clearly what the actual relationship really is in the present. Men always know what they want; they're just not willing to share that information with you prior to the relationship. Men understand that women have appetite tendency to lay all of their cards out on the table from the beginning. This allows men to feed women with an empty spoon and pursue the relationship on their own terms. Remember, some men want to enjoy the benefits of being a husband while desiring and practicing the privileges of being a bachelor. He may profess his love for you, but in actuality, what he really loves is the way you love him. Remember, when you really love an individual, your actions become your words, and your words become only a symbol of your actions.

You can't have one foot in the tub and one foot out.
~Thelma Carswell, 1932–1987

Chapter 5

You Think You Know? You Have No Idea!

Sleeping With the Enemy

Most people have been in relationships that they thought would to be their last hurrah and would one day lead to marriage. Some relationships hit hard times, and couples get through them; however, that's not always the case.

Remember, someone can be with you, but not for you. Don't mistake motion for action or attendance for alliance. I've heard people say, "We've been through so much together, and that's why I can't get over this person or believe it's over." Never get caught up in how much time or money you feel you have wasted, for the value is not in the time spent but in the time saved. Forgive those whom you feel have taken advantage of your kindness, time, and money. If you don't, you will mourn forever, and forever is a very long time to give to someone who wasn't right for you in the first place. So many people are sleeping with the enemy and fail to realize that loving someone and truly having an alliance with your partner should come effortlessly.

He who loves more is the inferior and must suffer.
~Thomas Mann 1875–1955

20/20 Vision

When two people meet it's mostly what I call the "Matrix" (an optical Illusion). Most people present themselves with their best foot forward; however, time will always tell if they were "false advertising." If you value your time, as most people do, then don't let your hindsight be your 20/20 vision. I'm not saying that you should be a pessimist and not give a potential good person a chance, if we all did that, then no one would ever get past the first date, but I do challenge you to see past your lust, and focus on the character of the person you're dealing with. Remember, a person's character is ever more prevalent than what their opinions are on certain issues. When you allow yourself to see beyond the initial attraction and dig deeper, that's when you'll find your 20/20 vision. Once your vision is clear, you can make an assessment about whether to pursue the relationship and where you want to take it. Most people have more physical and material things in common than character traits. For example, two people may both love the life of luxury; however, one person embraces luxurious possessions to define who they are, and the other person appreciates exactly what they are—material things that will one day depreciate.

Scratch a lover and find a foe.
~Dorothy Parker, 1893–1967

Remember Who's on Your Team

Always remember who's on your team, and never forget that, deep down inside, you fully understand who's proven and who's unproven. Too many times, we as individuals will stray away from our relationships to fulfill our own self-emptiness. We begin to magnify problems that could have simple resolutions simply because we are afraid to face the harsh truth of our inadequate actions. This behavior does not serve our best interests, and in essence, it destroys our growth as individuals. The things we do to sabotage our relationships so that our partners can give us false validations for our cowardly exits will only add to our karmic failure, especially when we make these exits to pursue other interests that we know are wrong. Always acknowledge who's on your team at all times. Just because the grass seems greener on the other side doesn't mean its appearance is just. We all understand that storms are as prevalent in life as they are in nature, for the grass that has no roots will be washed away never to return again. It is only when the grass has grown roots that it will be able to stand firm through the natural storms of life and relationships and be beautiful once again. One should nourish our relationships with those who have been tested time and time again, instead of abandoning them.

The difference between us is that my family begins with me,
whereas yours ends with you.
~Iphicarates, c. 419–348 B.C.

Communication

Communication is fifty percent of the relationship; the other fifty percent is money and sex. Never cut the lines of communication. It's true that in a tense situation you may need to step back and gather your composure, but it is essential that you acknowledge the sensitivity of the problem and assure your partner that you will revisit the issue at hand in a calmer atmosphere and that you will not dismiss it as invalid or unworthy of your time. Even professional boxers need a time-out to regain their composure. It's ok to agree to disagree. No two people will see eye-to-eye in every situation. When we have misunderstandings, it is important that we allow our mates to clarify their positions clearly so that we don't misinterpret what they are saying.

There are people who instead of listening to what is being said to
them, are already listening to what they are going to say themselves.
~Albert Guinon, 1863–1923

When You Know, You Know

When asked the question, "Have you ever been in love?" most people say that they guess they have been. When you're in love with someone, it's not a feeling you will guess about at all. Most people get lust or infatuation confused with love. I wonder how many people who are in relationships and marriages are not in love but are in transactions with one another for the sake of security. When you are truly in love it consumes you from head to toe, and your actions come from your heart, resonating your love in all that you do for one another. When you love a person you never stop loving that person. Your actions for one another may be put on a long hiatus depending on the situation at hand, but the love never dies. You may fall out of lust, but you will never fall out of love.

Love and cough cannot be hid.
~George Herbert, 1593–1633

Choices

One of the greatest gifts of all is our God-given right to make choices. When you take away someone's choice in a relationship, you have assumed the role of their creator. The power to make our own decisions about life, liberty and the pursuit of happiness should not be clouded by deceit, lies and selfish behavior for our own gain. What we choose to do with our lives is our own choice, but when we make decisions for someone else without their knowledge, we have ultimately betrayed the trust we must have to maintain a healthy relationship. And deeper than that, we have ripped away the other person's God-given inheritance of choice.

Who gives you the right to take away with god has given.
~Anonymous

Chapter 6

Food for Thought

$$\equiv\equiv\equiv\equiv\equiv\equiv\equiv\equiv\equiv\equiv\equiv\equiv\equiv\equiv\equiv$$

I Am Your Friend First

When a man and a woman are truly the best of friends, there is nothing they can't overcome or become. Being a true friend costs you nothing, but the rewards of that friendship can last a lifetime When we put our greatest fears aside and step into each other's lives with the innocence and simple desires of childhood, when we give love where we see love and truly love one another purely and not as a transaction, then the essence of true friendship can be embraced without the fear of failure, but with the courage to overcome our greatest vulnerabilities as individuals. Love built on the foundation of true friendship can stand the test of time and the obstacles of life.

A true friend is one who overlooks your failures
and tolerates your success.
~Doug Larson, 1952–

Love, What a Beautiful Thing It Is

Love is a beautiful feeling; the way it makes you feel throughout your whole body is a miracle in itself. The reputation that it has from scorned lovers is blasphemy to something so pure. Love is not the problem in relationships that go wrong; people who use love to mask their erroneous behavior are the ones we should blame. Never stray away from a feeling that is so magical that if we all practiced it as a religion and not as an act of lust or deceit, we would live full of joy and prosperity. What a world that would be! Appreciate being in love. If you have loved and lost, look forward to the day when that feeling can be claimed again instead of marinating in the spoils of its departure.

To cheat oneself out of love is the most terrible deception;
it is an eternal loss for which there is no reparation,
either in time or in eternity.
~Soren Kierkegaard, 1813–1855

The Future is in Front of You

Some people find themselves in situations that could have been prevented from day one because their future was always right in front of them. What you consistently tolerate today is where you will find yourself tomorrow. Enduring through hard times or life altering events is one thing, but when the damage comes before the storm, it's time to re-asses your position. Do not linger in the state of procrastination because you dread change. Knowing what you have to do and doing it is two entirely different things. Be wise enough to know when things presented to you run deeper than your endurance. The future is always right in front of you, and it's up to you to choose it.

What men usually ask of God when they pray
is that two and two not make four.
~Anonymous

Hand Them Their Heart,
and Become an Unselfish Person

Understand that when you have another person's heart, it is the most delicate thing they could have given you. It is a part of themselves that is unrehearsed and unedited. Your first option is to love that person back as much as they love you and to rejoice in the very essence of love. If you are staring true love in the face and because of your own issues you cannot handle the relationship, then the noble thing to do is to hand that person's heart back to them and bow out gracefully. We all battle with the selfish and unselfish parts of our hearts. Most of us practice the selfish part with perfection, but it is the unselfish part that we must practice when we have someone else's heart.

No person was ever honored for what he received.
Honor has been the reward for what he gave.
~Calvin Coolidge, 1872–1933

As Time Passes, Will You?

It does you no good to dwell on old sorrows and things that were supposed to be but never materialized. When you began to look at your life, you must ask yourself, "Did I take enough chances on myself with love, relationships, and career choices?" When you limit the chances you're willing to take, you limit your success. Some people look up, and their life has passed them by because they spent too much time pondering whether they should take chances. Caution is good, but when you apply it to everything in life, you will learn that time waits for no one, not even the person with the good heart, the good job, etc. Time moves on, and you should move on as well with a new focus and a heart that is not afraid of failure, immune to disappointment and optimistic about love and all that it has to offer.

*If one could recover the uncompromising spirit of one's youth, one's
greatest indignation would be for what one has become.*
~Andre Gide, 1869–1951

Forget the Five-Carat Ring.
Give Me a Successful Marriage

Some people chase their perception of what they feel the perfect
marriage should consist of such as a five-carat ring and luxury cars.
Although the finer things in life are great to have, the foundation of
what marriage is built on should be even greater. Happiness is priceless.
Some people have the wedding of their dreams and the marriage of
their nightmares. Take time to build your foundation so that what is
built on that foundation is even stronger. Material things can never
replace the needs of human emotion such as happiness, respect, and
most of all honesty. I once overheard a women say she would never
get married unless the man had a five-carat ring in front of her, which
is sad because that woman's self-value was only five-carats. In that
same conversation, the woman she was talking to replied, "Forget the
five-carat ring. Just give me a successful marriage, and then one day
we can upgrade."

*Where there's marriage without love,
there will be love without marriage.*
~Benjamin Franklin, 1706–1790

Marriage Does Not Equal Comfort

Just because you're married doesn't mean that your mate automatically disappears from the eyes of the world. It may seem like a news flash to you, but you're not the only one in life who finds your mate attractive, intelligent, and desirable. Marriage does not equal comfort; it's a commitment between two individuals, and it requires work. It's important to be very supportive in everything your mate strives for. Always be your mate's biggest cheerleader. Never stop the compliments or lose those extra nerves that keep you on your p's and q's and ahead of the game. Remember that what you are no longer willing to do, someone else will be more than willing to do. Allow the expression of each other's deepest desires to be embraced with understanding and a willingness to please one another. If you're not willing to put the work in to keep your marriage alive and vibrant, then you have doomed your plans for growth and a lasting marriage.

It would be impossible to "love" anyone or anything one knew completely. Love is directed towards what lies hidden in its object.
~Paul Valery, 1871–1945

Thoughts Are Things

Thoughts are things, and everything you think you can manifest. Before your shirt was a shirt it was someone else's thought, and that thought was manifested into something tangible. The most frustrating thing to us as individuals is how to get from point A to point B. In anything that you are trying to achieve, whether it be a successful marriage or a relationship that leads to marriage, the key to it all is small victories. When a baby is learning to walk he or she may fall down after a few steps, but with each step comes a small victory. So many people go through bad relationships, and the energy that they give off will always keep them in a continuous cycle of attracting bad situations. Anything that you approach with negative energy will produce a negative outcome. Some people seek out the negative in others to fuel their own suspicious of guarantees. My grandmother always told me, The only thing in life that is guaranteed is death and taxes. Everything else is extra credit."

No One Loves the Farmer

Everyone loves the harvest, but no one loves the farmer. The fruits of a successful marriage or relationship take a lot of work, patience, and persistence. Some individuals approach a relationship with limitations on building with their partner the foundations that will make their relationship stronger. Your investment into a relationship is what you will reap from it. A few individuals may disagree with that statement by saying, "I worked hard in a relationship and reaped nothing out of it." In those situations, the only reward received is a lesson. Every lesson is a blessing. What you've learned from that experience is to recognize the red flags that often appear before the experience. If you were a good person in the relationship, don't hide those qualities in your next relationship and replace them with bitterness. Always put your best foot forward, and never stop being who you are. The energy you waste trying not to be yourself is not worth it.

Happiness is beneficial for the body
but it is grief that develops the powers of the mind.

marcel proust 1871-1922

No Vision Equals a Dead-End Street

Some people have not a clue in the world about what they want or where they're going in life. There are certain questions that you should always ask people when you meet them. Where do you see yourself in five years? What steps are you taking to get there? What are some things that you do to make yourself happy? What are some negative things about yourself that you would love to change? What are some good things about yourself that you are extremely proud of?

When a person has no vision, they are blind to what they want for themselves. If you enter a relationship with someone like this, you will find yourself following someone who has no direction and will only lead you to a dead end street. If someone is taking the necessary actions to pursue their goals, this act alone shows that they have a level of vision and direction for their future. If someone knows how to make him or herself happy, they won't look to you to create their own happiness. Instead, they will be able to produce it within themselves. You will begin to read a person's sincerity when asking those questions. If the answers begin or end with "but," then you will come to the understanding that they are not being honest with themselves, so how do you expect them to be completely honest with you? When people are able to honestly admit their faults, they are on the path to correcting them. When people have something about themselves that they are proud of, they won't envy your accomplishments.

People often say that this or that person has not yet found himself.
But the self is not something one finds, it is something one creates.
~Thomas Szasz, 1920–

Chapter 7

Application of Advice: Part 2

Advice for Women

Men hate confrontation, so you may encounter their many creative ways of avoiding what you want to address. When this occurs, the best way to address the situation is to pull the emotion out of your approach. If you do this, your need for connection will be met, and you will get the answers that you need to move forward. There is a certain time and place for everything and the time and place in which you choose to discuss what's on your mind can determine the outcome of the situation. You get more with honey then you do with haste. In any situation, cooler heads always prevail. Remember, men don't deal with emotions very well, and a lot of men are really handicapped when it comes to expressing their emotions at the proper time. As a woman who understands when and how to communicate your feelings, you will prevail in getting a positive communication and connection. This will not only enhance your level of creativity in the relationship, but it will also save you some emotional turmoil.

Women prefer to talk in two's, while men prefer to talk in three's.
~Gilbert Keith Chesterton, 1874–1936

Advice For Men

You're never going to get everything you desire from one person, so it's up to you to be realistic and separate your needs from your wants. If you get eight out of ten things that you ask for, you're hitting home runs. If you're looking at longevity in a relationship, then there are some things you can live with and some things you can live without. As men, having options is our greatest gift, but it's also our greatest curse. The man who chooses many ends up with none. What you're lacking within yourself you need to fulfill on your own and not look for another person to validate each of those feelings or desires. If you want a freak in the bed and a lady as well, don't get mad if she doesn't do windows or dishes! If she's all of the above, then hold onto her, for that is what you would call a rare gem.

A woman we love rarely satisfies all of our needs,
and we deceive her with a woman whom we do not love.
~Marcel Proust, 1871–1922

Advice for Women

There are more women than men, so when looking for Mr. Right, ask yourself what makes you different from every other woman? So many women think that certain accomplishments are a plus for attracting a man—college educated, independent, etc.—but that's not the slam-dunk for men that most women think it should be. The women who go against the grain and don't follow all the rules are usually the ones who succeed in getting the men of their dreams. Things like paying when you go out to dinner or indulging in some of the man's favorite hobbies are sometimes viewed negatively as not what a woman should do. For example, if he asks you out, he should pay. But to men, these unorthodox acts alone separate you from the rest of the pack. Many women approach their relationship with a potential mate too cautiously because they are afraid of being taken advantage of. They think, "If I pay for dinner or do something against the grain, he's going to think I'm a pushover." But don't be so afraid. Your intelligence will always kick in when you get a jerk who's not worthy of your time or energy. Not all men are jerks, though, and sometimes a fifty-dollar dinner is cheaper than a three year heartbreak.

We often make people pay dearly for what we think we give them.
~Contesse Diane [Marie Josephine de Suin de Beausac], 1829–1899

Advice for Men

Haven't you ever heard that it's the little things that count? For most women, it really is the little things that count, except for your finances. It's always good to pay close attention to your mate and act on the things that are small but mean so much—having her coffee ready when you're both on your way to work, really sitting down and listening to her if she's had a bad day or just in general. The little things add up to the big things and so on and so on. The majority of men don't pay attention to the details of their relationships with women, and that's why the cracks in the relationships lead to others filling those voids. What you're not willing to do, the next man will be willing to do.

Anything will give up its secrets if you love it enough.
~George Washington Carver, c 1864–1943

Advice For Women

Most women will want for a man what he doesn't want for himself. I call this syndrome "maternal dysfunction", and many women suffer from it. It's natural for women to be strategic in planning a relationship, but in doing this, most women are too naïve. They often end up giving men the very map they need to control the relationship to their own benefit. I strongly advise women never to initiate a relationship being too transparent in an effort to display how forthright and honest they are. There is a big difference between understanding internally exactly what you want the relationship to mature into and expressing those thoughts aloud, only to have him play along. Remember, it's easier for people to be who they really are than to be who they're not. When you fully understand this concept, then you can navigate thoroughly through potential candidates. Don't be afraid to ask him the kinds of questions that will make him think long and hard before he answers. From those answers, you can make your mental notes about where he's at in his life without giving off an emotional reaction that will make him change his tune to match your reaction. Not every man is at the same point in his life as you are in yours. Some may be ready to settle down when you're not ready and vice versa. Men will really always tell you who they are in an indirect way by their opinions on certain things and the way they handle certain situations, etc. Read between the lines because what you see is definitely what you get. Don't make excuses for behavior that you would be ashamed to discuss with someone else. If the foundation is not stable, then what you build is sure to collapse.

Problems are messages.
~Shakti Gawain, 1948–

Advice for Women

A closed mouth never gets fed. Stop assuming that men know exactly what you're thinking because they don't. You should be clear about what you require in a relationship and not assume that a man's reaction to a certain situation will be the same as yours. Men generally don't react in ways that are obvious to women. Men are black and white with no grey areas. Assumption with a man is the worst way you can approach improving your relationship and getting what you want from it.

To assume with out direct communication
is that of a ship sailing with out a destination.
~Abgazd Hovedada 1972–

Advice for Men

It's the little things that count with women. So many men make the mistake of thinking that they have to go out and conquer the world in order to be appreciated by women when in fact, doing the little things that will help her get through the world is where you conquer her. When you take the time to really pay attention and listen to what she is saying you'll stop feeling clueless. Figuring out what she wants will no longer seem as difficult as finding the cure for cancer. The key word is "listening". Use the information that she's giving you as the tools you can use to be more attentive to the relationship.

Men's vows are women's traitors.
~William Shakespeare, 1546–1616

Advice for Women

Every man has his faults, but never settle for faults that you can't live with. Some women would love to take a little out of each man they have known and create the perfect lover, but that's neither realistic nor desirable. Be very true to yourself when dealing with any man whom you're considering for a permanent position in your life. Make sure he wants for his woman what he would want for himself. Accepting imperfection doesn't mean taking a back seat to blatant disrespect, etc. It means for you to mark your position from the beginning of the relationship. It means asking yourself what is tolerable and what is not and whether you can live with one or two imperfections for the rest of your life or whether you are settling for what you know in your heart will be the very demise of your happiness.

It is assumed that a woman must wait, motionless, until she is wooed.
That is how the spider waits for the fly.
~George Bernard Shaw, 1865–1950

Chapter 8

Rules of Engagement

Rules for a successful relationship

➤ Never yell unless there is a fire.

➤ Never go to bed angry

➤ Always go to bed naked because if you're angry, you'll work out your issues in the middle of the night.

➤ Your first romantic efforts are usually your tools for longevity. Never throw them away.

➤ Always renovate the structure of your relationship. Nothing new can ever grow in old soil.

➤ If one person is finance, someone else has to be management. Each individual should respect the other's job.

➤ Sacrifice things that are reasonable for the benefit of the relationship.

➤ Give from your heart and never from your mouth, for the heart has no mouth for speaking, only actions for doing!

➤ Listen to your partner, don't just hear them! When you are truly listening you are not thinking of your rebuttal or contemplating your defense.

➤ Want for your partner what you would want for yourself.

➤ Saying that you are working on your bad habits is just an excuse for delaying the change. The cure is simple: change the bad habit.

➤ Keep the arguments clean and the sex dirty.

Communication is key. Democritus of Abdera said it best: "To do all the talking and not willing to listen is a form of greed."

Love between two individuals should be as effortless as scratching your head or opening a door, but in life there will be things outside of that love you have for each other that will obstruct and sometime confine what should be a simple effort. When this happens, usually you will have to work harder at loving each other.

Stay in Your Lane

Life is about balance. I once heard a woman express that some men can't handle a strong independent woman. To some extent, I agree with that statement; however, in my species' defense, I think that a lot of women, for a long period of time, have had to step it up and assume roles that were never expected of women before, especially if they are single mothers. Although some men think that strong women are a little too much, the majority of men appreciate them. The key is staying in your lane. When you approach the relationship with a team spirit, the "ME" turns into "WE". Trusting your mate to do his or her job in the relationship is a huge factor because the gratification of trust can be enough for your mate to go beyond his or her potential. There is always more then one way to do something in life. Make room for mistakes from your partner but not to the tune of permanent failure. Independent woman and men need to look at their mates not as accessories to their relationships but as an intricate, needed piece of the balance in a happy and healthy relationship

It is a golden rule not to judge men by their opinions
but rather by what their opinions make of them.
~Georg Christoph Lichtenberg, 1742–1799

When You Forget Your Place, You Have No Place

Forgetting your position in a relationship can cost you that relationship. In any relationship, the key is balance. Most of us forget our place and do things that are out of place and harmful to the other person. We then expect that person to honor our place as if we've never compromised it from day one. People are not ignorant about the things they do in relationships. It is in our human nature to test boundaries to see just how far we can go with other people. Kindness can easily be taken for weakness, and making excuses for others only champions their actions and encourages them to continue on a path of non-growth and non-self-accountability. Ask yourself where you draw the line for happiness, growth, and spiritual enlightenment.

The Truth Will Set You Free

The truth will set you free. Being comfortable with being a liar is an entrapment within yourself that is mentally and spiritually destructive. For some people, not being honest to avoid confrontation only makes matters worse. Lying only smoothes over the immediate problem; it does not cure the problem within yourself. It all starts with you and what you as an individual can do to improve your character and to make your reality match the way you want to be perceived.

Truth is the cry of all. But the game of few.
~George Bishop Berkeley, 1685–1753

Love is Work

Some people don't understand that love is constant work. The energy going out has to match the energy coming in. When you consistently nourish the relationship with positive attributes, the rough patches aren't as rough as they would be otherwise. Ask yourself, "What can I do to make the relationship better? How can I, each and every day, approach my union unselfishly?" When two people adopt this attitude, then no one ever feels empty inside or tires from giving until he or she has no more. Want for your partner what you want for yourself. Nourishing the relationship builds your union with each other. Love never gives out or gives up; only the person claiming it does.

There can be no peace of mind in love,
since the advantage one has secured is never anything
but a fresh starting-point for further desires.
~Marcel Proust, 1871–1922

Let Your Actions Be Your Words

A lot of people speak on their actions but seldom act on their actions in a relationship. When you love someone, it is important that your actions be your voice; it's what you do and not what you say that makes the difference. Saying "I love you" is very important as well, but showing someone that you love them means so much more.

Gratitude is a useless word.
You will find it in a dictionary but not in life.
~Francois, Duc de La Rochefoucauld, 1613–1680

Please Bring Your "A" Game

There is something profound about bringing your "A" Game toward everything you approach. Stop waiting to see what the other person is going to do, and just be the best "you" that "you" can be. There is no extra charge for being yourself. We've all sometimes been so disappointed that the mere thought of bringing our "A" Game seems overwhelming and somewhat cheesy, but unenthused energy breeds and attracts the same.

We have no more right to consume happiness without producing it
than to consume wealth without producing it.
~George Bernard Shaw, 1856–1950

Know How to Make Yourself Happy

Some people spend their whole lives looking for love in all the wrong places and faces only to come up empty. You should always take the time to know what makes you happy and to do things for yourself that make you happy. Self-perseverance is the first rule of nature, and catering to yourself allows you to be a better person. It instantly helps you to recognize what it is that you as a person can do to fulfill those empty spaces within yourself with true happiness rather than with trivial pursuits. When you know what makes you happy, you will never look to someone else for those feelings. Any happiness that other person can bring to the relationship will be considered extra credit.

We seek our happiness outside ourselves,
and in the opinion of people we know to be flatterers, insincere,
unjust, full of envy, caprice and prejudice.
~Jean de La Bruyere, 1645–1695

Take the Blinders Off

Some people have blinders on in their lives that they will never take off. When you can only see one direction, then you can't adapt to the world or to your relationship as it changes. There is no relationship that stays the same; if it does, it's a relationship without growth, and when there is no growth, there is only demise that awaits in the future. There are many things in life you may not agree with; however, understanding another point of view will help you be more diplomatic in approaching new ventures in your relationship. Taking the blinders off will help you pick better battles and fully receive what your partner is trying to express to you within reason. Some things are not within reason, and for those issues you have to stand your ground. However, when two people love each other, the simplest things can be hard to deal with because they are dealing with a lot of emotions like pride. An open mind leads to an open heart.

He who is outside his door
already has the hard part of his journey behind him.
~Dutch proverb

Trial and Error

Nobody approaches a relationship with all of the answers, and no person or relationship is perfect. The things you learn help you get better at each relationship that you are involved in. The key word is *learning*. Really learning from past mistakes and successes is all a part of trial and error. When you truly learn from your experiences, you can allow yourself to grow. Often we find ourselves in situations where we tell ourselves, "It's too hard to get out of this and just walk away." But some relationships are so unhealthy for the body, mind, and spirit that we need to get out of them immediately. Other relationships can prosper into something beautiful with hard work. Don't be afraid to be the best that you can be by taking chances on yourself.

Everybody wants to be somebody: Nobody wants to grow.
~Johann Wolfgang von Goethe, 1749–1834

Romance Without Finance is a Nuisance

Most marriages and relationships are destroyed over finances; the fact is that money plays a very important part in building a healthy relationship. A lot of people like to approach relationships with the attitude that love will conquer everything, but the fact of the matter is that love doesn't pay the electric bill or keep food on the table. Dating and marriage should be the last thing on your mind if your finances aren't in order. When two people come together, the union should be stronger, not weaker. If you are in a marriage and you're going through money difficulties, then it's time to come together as a team and re-work your finances so that you can get back on your feet. Money won't buy happiness—that's something you just can't pay for—but money does provide choices that are often denied without it.

Money is like a sixth sense
without which you cannot make a complete use of the other five.
~William Somerset Maugham, 1874–1965

♥ ♥ ♥

Chapter 9

Get the Memo and Get Going

Get a Life

S ome people who surround us have no life of their own so they relish other people's romantic mishaps. Think about that ex-girlfriend who never has anything good to say about the person you're dating or the people who are so holier-than-thou that they send you to hell and back when you don't do what they think is right for your life. This action is simple—there are some people you have to tell to just get a life and stay out of yours.

> *The people who are regarded as moral luminaries*
> *are those who forego ordinary pleasures themselves*
> *and find compensation in interfering with the pleasures of others.*
> ~Bertrand Arthur William Russell, 1872–1970

Let Go and Move Forward

Many of us have found ourselves in situations where we have to forgive our mate for something they did that hurt our feelings. Some things are forgivable and some things are not. It depends on your tolerance level for the act itself. If you know in your heart that you can't get past what the person has done, then do yourself and the other party a favor and move on. However, if you and your partner have enough invested in each other that the relationship can be salvaged, then you must leave the old behind and move forward.

Once a person has forgiven someone
they must not reheat their sins for breakfast.
~Marlene Dietrich, 1904–1992

Guiding Light

Most often we as individuals wear a mask that can be so heavy that the need and desire for our true colors to be exposed can turn into something so drastic and unkind, it takes more energy to not be yourself then it does to be who you are. Don't be disappointed when people are not accepting of who you are and of the unique light you have to bring to this world. We are not all at the same level, and you should never lower your light to accommodate the insecurities of others. We are all guided by that internal light to be who we really are, and it's up to us to follow it.

To others we are not ourselves but a performer in their lives cast for
a part we do not even know that we are playing.
~Princess Elizabeth Bibesco, 1897–1945

No Heat to Warm the Heart

Some people are just so cold-blooded that they can drag us into their world of disarray if we allow them to. People who inflict pain upon others are lacking the heat of the soul that warms the heart. Individuals who act like this are seldom happy with themselves, and no matter what you do for them, they will never be happy. If you find yourself involved with a person like this, the best door to take is the exit. People who really love you would never want to hurt you.

Those who do not feel pain seldom think that it is felt.
~Dr. Samuel Johnson, 1709–1784

Marriage is not Prison

The marriages that survive and thrive are those that allow fantasies to exist and they encourage the exploration of different dimensions of the union. Is it important to allow your partner to be fully honest with you without being morally judged and condemned? Action and communication are two totally different things. When people can keep their individualism within a marriage, then a true and successful marriage will exist.

It takes a loose rein to keep a marriage tight.
~John Stevenson

It Takes Three to Make One

Years ago my uncle was getting married, and he told me that two people couldn't hold a marriage together. I was a little bit shocked because I thought, "You just got married last week, and you want to start cheating already?" I asked him what he would do if his new wife ever caught him cheating. He laughed and said, "I'm not talking about cheating on my wife. That is absurd." He then sat me down and explained that when two people come together, there must be some spirituality between the two of them to keep the union together as one.

He went on to say that when a person is getting their hair braided, in order for the braid to become one braid and stay together, a third element must always be implemented so that the two become one tight unit.

So heavy is the chain of wedlock that it needs two to carry it, and sometimes three.
~Alexander Dumas, fils 1824–1895

God Bless the Child That Has Its Own

"Mama may have, and Papa may have, but God bless the child that has its own." In any relationship, you should always have something of your own; this promotes a healthy individual as well as a healthy team player. When you embark on your own accomplishments and bring those accomplishments into your relationship, the unity of your relationship is reinforced with confidence and support for one another. Everything that you want may not come as fast as you would like, but when you keep accumulating small victories, you will soon achieve your final goal.

Do not completely rely on another human being however dear. We meet life's greatest tests alone.
~Agnes Campbell Mac Phail, 1890–1954

Walk Away with Dignity and Gain Respect

When a relationship goes wrong, the worst thing you can do is to live in deceit to remedy the problems of your unity. It is better to approach your partner with dignity and express your intentions than to flounder in deceit or drive your current situation into a hellish experience until the other party concedes Although facing adversity in a relationship is not easy, the dignity of dealing with the situation honestly can only be respected. Even if it is not appreciated at first because emotions are high, the seeds that you sow will indeed be the same growth you will revisit at one time or another.

It requires as much caution to tell the truth as to conceal it.
~Baltasar Gracian, 1601–1680

Shared Feeling from Focus Group

I had given my heart and soul throughout the relationship only to feel very empty afterwards. It was only after I was out of the relationship that I realized I never was getting back what I put into it emotionally. He often accused me of being an emotional drama queen, but it was his non-emotional actions that drove me crazy. I showed and told him that I loved him very often only to receive what I perceived as non-appreciative reactions. What I learned was that his way of showing affection was very different from my way of showing affection and that either I had to adjust or he would have to really step up and give me what I needed emotionally to continue to be the best person I could be. However, this thinking came after I was out of the relationship and had moved on with my life. What the situation taught me was that I have to be totally honest with myself and know going into a relationship that having the most important things in common, such as emotional support, will give the relationship its common ground. When you build a relationship from the inside out, it tends to work in your favor because you get familiar with the very intriguing parts of the individual you're dealing with.

He who loves more is the inferior and must suffer.
~Thomas Mann, 1875-1955

Chapter 10

What is Your Definition of Team Work?

Agendas

When two people meet, they each have an agenda. The difficulty comes when the two agendas are not compatible. Hidden agendas cause damaging surprises for couples who are in relationships. There is someone for everybody, and those with like-minded agendas should be together. If you are a person who wants to be married with children, you should know that there is no chance that someone who doesn't want children will bend for the sake of the relationship. Your ways and ideas that you express to someone that you have in interest will not change someone who is not already seeking that same road and has no plan to get there. People are who they are. Mean-spirited people don't change into nice people—they just become repressed versions of themselves, always on the brink of becoming who they once were.

All that we do is done with an eye to something else.
~Aristotle, 384–322 B.C.

Cool, Calm and Collected

Being cool is a state of mind not an act of being. If you have to think about being cool, you're not cool. Calm is more than not being scared or nervous—it's knowing how to hold it together when life throws you an unexpected curve ball. Being collected is pulling it all together even when you don't have all the answers to your problems or life's obstacles. These three life lessons are what may be instilled in a person when they seek it.

If you want to be witty, work on your character
and say what you think on every occasion.
~Mari-Henri Beyle Stendhal, 1783–1843

What Can Work for You?

The majority of people who are dating are looking for Mr. and Mrs. Right. They don't exist. Who does exist is Mr. and Mrs. Work. The "right" person for you is someone who can work well with your individual strengths and weaknesses. Everyone we meet will not have every quality that we need in an individual, but if you can get what works for you, then you can move forward and progress toward building a happy and healthy relationship. If you are dead-set on getting everything you need from one individual, then please be prepared to be by yourself.

Grab a chance and you won't be sorry for a might have been.
~Arthur Mitchell Ransome, 1884–1967

Single Dating

I don't think that people who are dating should feel entitled to the benefits of being in a relationship. This is a time when two individuals are getting to know each other, and the approach to dating should be one of independence. If you go out to dinner on your first date, the bill should be split in half; if the chemistry is there, then one person covers for the first and the other for the second. So many people approach dating with the same rules their parents had when the times were different. You're either one way or the other way. If you're a woman and feel that the old-fashioned way of dating is that a man pays for all of the dates, then you can't get mad if he drops his laundry off for you to do—he's just going by old-fashioned rules, too, where the woman does all the laundry. A lot of people want the benefits of a wife or husband with the privileges of a bachelor or bachelorette. You need to realize that you can't have it all one way, and in order to stay balanced you must practice balance so that you're not giving more of yourself then your mate deserves.

Nothing is so good as it seems beforehand.
~George Eliot [Marian Evans Cross], 1819–1880

Against All Odds

I've always admired those love stories of triumph over defeat. They confirm for me that true love can and always does overcome all obstacles if you just let it.

When Nelson Mandela was released from prison after twenty-seven years behind bars because he wanted to end apartheid in his country, I marveled at the spirit of his wife, Winnie Mandela, who fought for his freedom every day of his imprisonment and finally saw him released and elected president of the country.

I really feel that in a relationship, one must look at the heart of the individual and build from that. When you have the heart for anything in life, the impossible becomes possible. I think that everyone who enters your life teaches you something—it's up to you to learn from those teachings. Throughout my dating life, I've learned the lessons that were given. Some of those lessons took a repeat session in order for me to get the complete lesson, but nonetheless, I have learned all of those lessons and have applied them to my everyday life, not just my dating life. I think that the hardest thing in dating is to build a fortress around yourself because of your past negative experiences. Ask yourself if you would ever attempt to purchase anything sight unseen. I've learned to embrace my failures along with my triumphs—it's the order of balance, and it teaches us to embrace all sides of love, life and relationships. I've encouraged a great deal of people who are dating to look at what they bring to the table as opposed to what they can take from it. When you have so much to give, your eye for receiving should not stray from the art of giving. I understand that the enthusiasm for giving your best can be terribly diminished after each disappointment, but no good deed put out into the universe goes unanswered. It may not be answered directly by the person who benefited from your good deeds but it will come, and when it does it's on you to recognize it and proceed forward to receive back the gifts you've put out into the universe. I wish I could understand the full dynamics of why some people are who they are, but I learned a long time ago that you can't change anyone else's behavior; however, you can change your own behavior. I have learned to stop doubting my instincts for the cheap trade of curiosity, (I wonder what's behind door number two?). I now know that people show us who they really are far sooner than we would expect and that if we just learn to listen to our inner sensory guides that tell us what is good and what is not good, then the lessons of the past will not have to be repeated.

Dating Frustration

I woke up not on the wrong side of the bed but on the frustrating side of reality. I felt like deleting every meaningless number out of my phone and I did just that. "Are you sure you want to delete? Hell, yes!" It seemed to me that everyone wanted something from me, and no one had anything to offer. I wasn't talking about material things, but spiritually, emotionally, mentally, and physically. Why couldn't I just find the perfect person who meets all my simple requirements, and why can't we just live happily ever after. Were my requirements that much? Suddenly I began to doubt what I should really be looking for, and I started to ask myself, "Am I asking too much of one person?" I wanted beauty, brains, a sense of humor, a sense of adventure, a revolutionary, a business mind-set, patience, persistence, and confidence. I wanted all of the things that I am and all of the things that I am not in one person. Was that realistic? The more frustrated I became over trying to find the perfect woman, the more I began to learn that I wasn't perfect myself, and I couldn't ask of someone what I myself fell short of. I decided that I would look for the things from a woman that I need to be happy, because happiness is the most important thing.

Never let anyone steal your joy it's your gift from God.
~Mabel Nottingham, 1919–1948

Focus

Sometimes when we meet someone, we look past the things we need to focus on because of our initial attraction to the person. Take a moment to step back from your lust, and look, evaluate and focus on who you're dealing with. Do you have the same values on certain things? Ask those scenario questions, and with their own words people will tell you who they are and where they stand on certain issues. It's up to you to keep the focus on where they stand and where you want to be standing. Those high hopes of things going your way are merely an illusion of the heart and mind because your judgment is clouded by lust. Everyone knows what they want. Some are just not bold enough to express it or honest enough to really tell you, so learn to read between the lines. Be realistic, and most of all be true to yourself.

We prove what we want to prove,
and the real difficulty is to know what we want to prove.
~Emile Auguste Chartier, 1868–1951

Chapter 11

Keep on Keeping on

Know When to Say No

Sometimes as soon as you meet a person you will know if you are very fond of them or not. If you are fond of them, then naturally your instincts to put your best foot forward will kick in. But know your limits, especially if the person does not seem as interested in pursuing the relationship as you are. Those excuses—"Let me warm up to you," etc.—are just that, excuses. People know what they want, and they will put their best foot forward as well. Don't allow your kindness be your weakness by investing large amounts of time entertaining a person who doesn't serve your best interests. Know when to say, "This is unhealthy for me to pursue. It's something that will eventually drain me emotionally."

> *Life is not long, and too much of it must not pass*
> *in idle deliberation how it shall be spent.*
> ~Dr. Samuel Johnson, 1709–1784

Love Is Not a Noun

Love is not a noun, it's a verb, and verbs are actions. Too many of us depend on the word "love" and all that it stands for to sustain us through our relationships instead of taking the time and remembering the actions that lead us to the feeling of love. When you divert from those actions, you have totally deviated from the loving path. Those feelings of how you used to feel will ultimately arise because you haven't replaced what you've depleted. A car can only go so far without gasoline, and when all of the gas is gone, you'll find yourself suddenly pushing the car based on your history together, and then as you approach a hill the weight of the car will suddenly become a burden. To avoid this burden, all you have to do is pull over, put your hazards on, assess the problem, fill it up with gas, and continue your journey while enjoying the ride.

For Your Consideration

The best things in life are free, and consideration is one of them. The everyday world we live in promotes such a singular lifestyle that a lot of individuals only care about their own welfare and existence. When you're dealing with someone who doesn't have the slightest consideration for you, you are experiencing what is to come, the prequel to the sequel in the devout art of selfishness. Look, and don't be afraid to challenge someone's habits around consideration because those habits are the standards by which you measure their character as a person with whom you intend to have a relationship. Self-centered people never stop being self-centered; they just learn how to better conceal their selfish ways. When you learn that consideration and self-perseverance are two totally different things and that one can love oneself and extend that self-love to others through unselfish contributions to the relationship, then you will understand that consideration is the greatest thing that you can bring to any relationship.

The Pursuit of Happiness

Your income is your outcome. When you pursue happiness with the unjaded enthusiasm—as if you've never fallen off the bicycle of love—then the energy with which you approach each potential relationship will increase your chances of a positive outcome. Thoughts are things, and everything you think you can manifest. We get so caught up in what we directly invest our time in, never realizing that sometimes it's the indirect that awaits us in the end. A farmer may plant a thousand seeds in a vast field, and the most prized plant may never grow to its expected potential. Now the farmer has two choices: either keep planting with the same love and a greater appreciation for the attempt, or continue with a hopeless attitude and energy that defeats his intentions.

Men's passions are so many roads by which they can be reached.
~Luc de Clapiers de Vauvenargues, 1715–1747

Do You Really Want Honesty?

Be careful about what you ask for because you might just get it. Ask yourself if you really want an honest person in your life. Then ask yourself how many times you lie to yourself. How honest are you with yourself? If your answer is that you are less honest than you would like to be, then you are one of those people who doesn't really want honesty. There are no grey areas when it comes to honesty; either you're honest or you're not.

Truth is the cry of all, but the game of few.
~George Bishop Berkeley, 1685–1753

Don't Cut Your Nose Off

So many of us have been through long-term relationships and marriages where a microwave mentality sets in—we want what we want instantly, and if that doesn't come when we expect it, embracing romance is not up for discussion. Knowing what you want and recognizing those qualities should not be a frustrating process; it should be a relaxed state of being. When you display a microwave mentality toward getting to know someone, you unknowingly thwart any chances of success in having a meaningful relationship. Allow yourself to enjoy others and what they have to offer as opposed to what you expect them to offer. What you so ferociously command can be viewed by others as demands. You get more with honey then with haste. When you throw your hands up in frustration and say, "It's my way or the highway," more often than not, you will be headed to the highway by yourself. Always remember that the chances you don't take are the aspirations you forfeit.

Calamities are of two kinds: misfortune to ourselves,
and good fortune to others.
~Ambrose Bierce, 1842–c. 1914

The Illusionist

Every soul on earth is hidden by some kind of mask. When you ask people to be themselves and take off their masks, you are asking them to face their best qualities and their most painful vulnerabilities. You must ask yourself whether you can love the core of a person. Most people will never know the core of another person because of those fears that we all have of being judged. We are imperfect human beings, and we live in a world filled with illusions. Often the notion of unmasking for one another is unthinkable. But when you can get past the illusion of what you want a person to be and deal with the imperfections of who they are, you will have successfully entered the world of realism.

Life contains but two tragedies.
One is not to get your heart's desire; the other is to get it.
~George Bernard Shaw 1856–1950

You Inspire Me and I Encourage You

Thoughts are always things. Be bold and fearless in all that you do. Make the most of each day, and each day will make the most of you. Life is about great moments; have as many as you can. Let the pessimists be pessimists, and let the skeptics be skeptics—that's what the world calls balance. If everyone were as brilliant, sophisticated, and classy as you are, then the scales of this world would be unbalanced or grounded, never elevating to a balanced level. Obstacles in life are hurdles—jump over them. Doors that are shut are entries to a pathway—build your own door. You are God's finest work in his finest hour of creation. Shine as expected, succeed as you should, for I am blessed to have laid eyes upon you because you've inspired me, and I hope that these words have encouraged you to continue onward and upward leaving a trail for all who aspire to greatness to follow with the courage to create their own pathway in this world.

He who has begun has half done. Dare to be wise: Begin.
~Quintus Horatius Flaccus, 65–8 BC

The Little Things

Haven't you heard that it's the little things that count? Small gestures of kindness go a long way with people you are attempting to build a relationship with. If you take a different direction and add a more personal touch to whatever gesture you're doing, you will give the other person food for thought long after you have left their presence. We live such a singular lifestyle that personal interaction can often elude us. We forget those small acts of kindness that we should perform on a day-to-day basis. The pyramids were not built from the top down—they were built from the ground up with the smallest rocks as their base.

I Won't Entertain the Negative

I will be the ear that you need when you need someone to vent to or to just hear you out. I will be the shoulder you need to lean on in your time of need. But I will not entertain the consistently negative chatter that follows some people like a bad cloud. When you are truly blessed, take that blessing and give thanks for it. If you have a roof over your head, thank God. It may not be the roof you want, but it's a roof! You may not have the car you want, but if it gets you from Point A to Point B, thank God for it! When you entertain the negative, you invite all that comes with the negative.

What Are You Looking For?

Most women ask this very question, and a lot of guys think this question but dare not utter the words out loud. Learn to embrace growth from individuals instead of looking for what you want. Looking creates frustration when you don't get exactly what you're looking for in someone, and when you become frustrated, that frustration clouds your vision and can cause you to look past what you probably should embrace. Most people, when given a title, feel that they have to stop being who they really are and embrace the expectations that come with the title. Consistency doesn't start with a title—it starts within an individual. Having more responsibility doesn't make a person responsible. Learn to embrace growth and natural habit. It is easier for someone to be who he or she is then to be who he or she is not.

What we anticipate seldom occurs;
what we least expected generally happens.
~Benjamin Disraeli, Earl of Beaconsfield, 1804–1881

I Am You. You Are Me.

What you give effortlessly to any relationship should be received back without effort. The more you have in common with someone, the more success your relationship will have. Opposites don't attract, they detract because of their inability throughout their relationship to see eye-to-eye on subjects that are within reason and beneficial to the relationship. It is always necessary to refill what you give out as an individual without having to ask or insinuate your needs. People find it easier to be who they are than to be who they are not. You can't make a person be a giving person if he or she is naturally not that way. When something is unnatural for a person, the burden of going against the grain will eventually be too much for them to handle, and you could be left in shambles. Recognize yourself in the other person so that it will be easier for you to parallel each other's efforts.

Independence

Please don't confuse co-dependence with independence. If you bought the car and can't afford it, you're not independent. If you go to a night club without money looking for someone else to buy you a drink, you are not independent, you're inadequate. If you're over twenty-five and still living at home, turning your parents' basement into your first apartment, and hoping that opportunity and your future will come knocking at the door, you are not independent. If you go out to dinner, and the other person pays, and you don't even attempt to leave the tip, you are not independent. Independent people have a certain respect and pride that they uphold—they would be ashamed to get something for nothing. Independent people don't wear their status on their arm or even sing it in a song because they're too busy being independent. Independent people will never tell you what they need—they will ask you what you need. If you're co-dependent instead of independent, then realize that, and stop claiming a status that you are not ready for, or in some cases, do not even desire.

Chapter 12

Stand for Something or Fall for Anything

Know When to Fold 'Em

There are some people in life who will cheat on you, use you, and disrespect you; then when you've finally seen the light at the end of the tunnel and gotten out of the situation, they will turn around and blame you for hurting them. People like this will ask of you what they are not willing to ask of themselves—loyalty, kindness, respect. If you have a big heart, and the person in question knows this, they will continue to play on your heart's desire and manipulate you into continuing on a self-destructive path that, in the end, will only hurt you. You, as a good person, have to quickly realize that you can't save everyone because not everyone wants to be saved. This advice is really important for women because they carry that motherly instinct. they want to come to the rescue or make a bad situation better, and they end up finding themselves in situations that drain the goodness and life right out of them only to have them miss their real blessing when it comes along.

Leave Your Bills at Home

A lot of people carry a tremendous number of previously accumulated bills when it comes to their love lives. Learn to leave those bills at home, or better yet, trash them entirely. No one wants to be responsible for another person's bills. Stop going into a new situation thinking that you're entitled to certain things from the new person that you didn't get from the previous person. No one owes you anything except you. Yes you. Don't expect others to give you what you're not able to give yourself. Self-esteem—it's called self-esteem. Self-sufficiency—that means you. Self-love—that means love yourself. Stop the dangerous cycle of looking for someone else to validate those things that you, and only you, can validate. When you learn to leave your previous bills at home and to move forward with a clean slate, your outlook for romance will blossom.

It Takes Two to Tango

All too often when a relationship goes sour because someone was cheating in the relationship, the person who was betrayed goes after the third party and not the person who betrayed them. It takes two to tango, and a third party can only do what the other person allows them to do. I know that emotions often rule in these situations and that we can all make bad decisions when we're feeling betrayed. Sometimes, the mere thought of someone else benefiting from our misery is enough to send us into a murderous rage. But ask yourself, if you were deceived, could the third party have been deceived as well? Who's the common denominator? You guessed it—the person who's the betrayer; and that's the person you need to deal with. Going after the third party makes you look like a complete fool, and looking like a fool is far worse than feeling like a fool. When faced with adversity, it's better to figure your way out of the situation then to dig your self deeper into it.

When the Chase is in A Circle

I think everyone loves a challenge in approaching something new, but when the challenge becomes constant, enthusiasm is quickly lost. Encouraging someone's efforts to build something with you creates motivation and excitement between the two of you. We can often get caught up in our own singular lifestyles and sometimes forget to reach back toward someone who's reaching forward toward us and is good for us. Learn to nourish those relationships that are less challenging and more spiritually encouraging—those relationships help us to be the very best person we can be. When the chase becomes a full circle, it will produce no benefits.

Bitter Medicine

There are people in this world who constantly serve bitter medicine in their relationships. These people have more self-love than love. Some people love the way you love them more than they love you. Stop confusing the love, energy and dedication that you give to sustain the relationship as a joint venture because it's not. When you cease to give, the relationship will no longer exist.

Rudeness is the weak man's imitation of strength.
~Eric Hoffer, 1902–1983

Expensive Purse but No Self-Worth

I see you walking down the street a mile away with that high priced purse. Is it Louis Vuttion, Gucci, Fendi? Who knows? The high priced purse struggles to keep its structure; it folds with every swing because there is not enough content inside to keep it from folding. The purse reminds me of its owner who is carrying it around like a trophy. Although your outside possessions are worth thousands of dollars, your internal make-up is impoverished. You don't have enough content inside of you to keep yourself from folding. Your worth begins from the inside out. What good is that high priced purse when the content in the purse is worthless? This is the same question you should ask yourself. Where does your self-worth begin?

Chapter 13

Application of Advice: Part 3

Advice for Women

The key to all men is appreciation. When you appreciate a man for the big things as well as the small things, his drive to put his best foot forward every time will be displayed unconsciously throughout the relationship. Men have always thrived on being appreciated since they were young boys showing their mothers how strong they were by taking out the garbage or risking being stung by bees while picking flowers for the number one woman in their lives.

Advice for Men

Never expect a woman to react to sex as you would. Sex for most women comes from emotions and not from lust. If a woman is bedding you that usually means that she likes you, and those feelings will only get deeper as the relationship begins to grow. Intimacy always deepens things with women because they are sharing a certain part of themselves with you as a connection. It is your duty to clarify your position so that there is no confusion later down the line. Most women think that men are mind readers, and since you are not a mind reader, you are left clueless when she snaps at you over dinner about your insensitivity regarding her feelings.

Advice for Women

Every man knows exactly what type of woman he's looking for. Men don't take a long time shopping in a store, and they don't take a long time to decide about marriage either. Please do not be duped into believing that old myth that men aren't capable of knowing exactly what they want because it's far from the truth. Men, for the most part, will not share their inner thoughts or their plans for the future, but please note that when you're in the future plans of a man, his actions will overpower his words. The best way to really unlock a man's actions is to pull the emotion out of your reactions when he gives you his unedited, honest opinions. This act alone will lure the man from behind his mask and unveil the answers you've been looking for.

You will never know till you try to reach them how accessible men are; but you must approach each man by the right door.
~Henry Ward Beecher, 1813–1887

Advice for Men

Despite all of the chaos that goes on between men and women, at the end of the day, a woman wants a man. She wants a man who can make her feel protected, loved and understood, even when she's going through her emotional times. Listening is one of the best things you can do to strengthen your relationship with a woman. Women are emotional beings, and they use every outlet they have to express themselves. Have you ever wondered why a woman is on the phone with her girlfriend for so long? It's because her girlfriend is a good listener. It's not so much what she's saying as it is that she's able to express herself. It doesn't cost you anything to lend an ear as she talks about what's important in her life; listening falls under the category of "small things". The more small things you do, the more appealing you become to a woman.

If a man hears much that a woman says, she is not beautiful.
~Henry S. Haskins, 1878–1957

Advice for Women

Men will only play the games you allow them to play. When you stand firm in your decision of any sort, he will respect you for the woman that you are. Make your tolerance level low for games and high for potential. If he's a good man with a minimal job but he's making the effort to improve his life and accomplish his goals, then your level of tolerance should be high. But if his career is everything you hoped for in a mate but his attitude doesn't reflect the love, time and effort that you've bought to the relationship, then it's time to move on. When you accept too much of a challenge from a man, you should prepare yourself for more challenges to come. Men will test your limits and push further each time because they understand that women deal with emotions and that they use their emotions to make the majority of their decisions!

When we feel that we lack whatever is needed to secure someone else's esteem, we are very close to hating him.
~Luc de Clapiers de Vauvenargues, 1715–1747

Advice for Men

What women find the most attractive in us we seldom recognize in ourselves. When a man has a lot of something, he may need less of it—unless it's money—and more of something else. Strength and confidence is what women look for in men, but they don't want a man to be so strong that he doesn't know how to be gentle or so confident that he becomes arrogant. When a man slows down and takes a serious look within, he will be able to make his weakness his strength.

Balance applies to everything in life.
~Edith Adadevoh 1905–2007

Advice for Women

If you gain a man's trust, you automatically get past his wall. Most men have a very hard time letting women close to their hearts because the fear of being hurt or the memory of past pain is too much to bear. For a man, the emotional trauma of heartbreak is not an easy thing to overcome, and it could ultimately throw them off physically or mentally. The same is true for woman; however, the advantage women have is that they tend to have better support systems. Women tend to have other women they can talk to about their heartbreaks, but men don't go to other men to talk about intimate problems in their relationships. There is rarely a bond between two men that allows them to feel secure pouring out their weaknesses, inhibitions, and failures. Every man sees himself has a winner in his own right; therefore, he doesn't believe he needs to listen or be coached on marriage, sex, finances, etc. Where woman embrace each other's opinions, men opt out. Instead they think, "If I can't fix it, I must be a failure." What needs to be validated with a man is that there is more then one way to skin a cat and that his way may not be the wrong way but one of many.

You never know till you try to reach them how accessible men are;
but you must approach each man by the right door.
~Henry Ward Beecher, 1813–1887

Advice for Women
Stop Enabling Him

So many women get involved with unmotivated men because their mothers taught them to tolerate unmotivated men. When you as woman don't break that cycle, you help breed the environment that festers this type of behavior. When you cater to a man who has been catered to all his life, you further enable him. What a man looks for in a woman is the traits of his mother but, when his mother is still enabling him as an adult, then you will never be able to compete or get a complete adult and mature man. There will be no incentive for him to have a backbone and instead his expectations of you will greatly increase.

The more help a person has in his garden, the less it belongs to him.
~William H. Davies, 1871–1940

Advice for Women

For men there is nothing more discouraging then a woman who seems unattainable. Some women haven't mastered the art of keeping the carrot in front of the mule to entice him to keep moving forward; if the mule thinks for a minute that the carrot is unattainable, he will stop moving. If you make yourself unattainable, the obstacles you have created to protect your feelings will backfire, and your initial goals for the relationship will never manifest. The key is balance and encouragement. Some women desire the benefits of an old-fashioned gentleman while rebuffing the work ethic of an old-fashioned lady. You can't mix apples and oranges. The rewards of hard work and diligence are what we people live for. Encouragement goes a long way, and making someone feel that their progression and efforts are appreciated sets the tone for the outcome you wish to achieve with the person you are considering having a relationship with.

In baiting a mousetrap with cheese,
always leave room for the mouse.
~Saki [Hector Hugh Monroe], 1870–1900

Advice for Men

Women are calculating thinkers. Everything you say or do is calculated in their heads to see if it adds up for their benefit or not. For some men this may seem selfish, but if you know anything about women, you'll realize that this way of thinking is a natural self-defense mechanism that extends to every female that has ever walked this earth, be it man or beast. Once you have a clear understanding of this natural mechanism, you won't interpret her natural wants as selfish. Females want the strongest males possible in all aspects of their lives for their own benefit as well as for the benefit of their offspring. As a man, it is in your best interest to work and build on your strengths and not worry about the cycle of women you may miss while you're doing so. There will always be a new cycle of women who will appreciate a strong man more than a weak one.

Advice for Women

When a man has to be given direction in every aspect of the relationship, then there is no challenge to you as a woman. Although some relationships may be easier for you because of your strong character or leadership, it does you no good to never challenge yourself in your capacity as a leader, mother, individual or wife. A plant can't grow if it is in the same pot it started out in as a seed.

The silliest woman can manage a clever man;
but it needs a very clever woman to manage a fool!
~Rudyard Kipling 1865–1936

Advice for Men

One thing that all women can agree on is that there is nothing more unattractive than a stupid man. A woman can deal with a man who has great potential but limited exposure. What a woman can't deal with is a man who claims victory in his stupidity. Women respect and admire a man who asks for guidance in a relationship—such as counseling going to counseling—much more than one who thinks that he has all of life's answers because he is a man. Remember, women love a man who's in control and not controlling. There is a difference, and smart men always exercise the right tactic.

When a stupid man is doing something he is ashamed of,
he always declares that it is his duty.
~George Bernard Shaw 1856–1950

Chapter 14

There Should Be No Excuses

Excuses and Failure

People often like the idea of doing better in their relationship, career, and overall lives. However, the personal barriers we place before our journeys leave us in a place of failure. Ask yourself whether you are tired of being tired? Are you tired of loosing? Your decisions about your life and future may seem selfish to those around you who are doing nothing with their own, but the only one who's holding you back from anything is you. The greatest gift we were all given as human beings was free will. Yes, God wants you to be in tune with him spiritually, but he also wants you to stop looking up and look in front of yourself. You have to be the voice of change for your life and your future no matter how bleak and uninviting the road ahead may look. Small victories amount to great accomplishments. Change is never easy, but it is necessary in order to obtain new growth and new life.

Rent Free

How long are you going to let those old heartbreaks and disappointments stay in your mind rent-free? Your spirit and your soul pay the price for those mishaps that you refuse to let go of because of you are unwilling to move forward. How can you ever expect to receive new love, prosperity, and direction when your heart is filled with negative rent-free issues from the past? Don't continue to let anything that is unproductive to your life and well-being live rent free while paying the price with your heart, health and sanity.

House of Failure

Excuses are nails that we use to build a house of failure. What a powerful statement for those people who want more for those in their lives then they want for themselves. The problems we repeatedly encounter in our relationships should not be met with nails to build a house of failure but with a bulldozer to clear the area for a house of success. When you want for someone what they, themselves, don't want, you've planted the seeds of failure. Every excuse you arm them with is another building block for a house of failure. It's always easier for people to be who they truly are than to be who they are truly not. When it's a struggle for a person to prove their goodness to you, then you should know that being good for you was not a natural priority for that person nor will they make the effort to progress. Instead, your relationship will progress toward that famous line, "It's not easy and were working on it." Someone can genuinely be a good person but not the right person for you, and the sooner you understand that, the less resentment you will acquire as a person who has endured the hardships of a relationship that received more than it gave, that hurt more than it healed.

Cheat Sheet

Sometimes we find ourselves in a transitional period in our relationship with the million-dollar question, "Should I stay or should I go? If only I had a cheat sheet on my predicament this would be an easy decision." Our ability to choose sometimes can be thwarted by fear of the unknown. When people don't have all the answers, it forces them to rely on themselves and on their substance as individuals. When you don't challenge your substance as an individual how can you ever clearly understand who you really are? Many great accomplishments have been marred by not knowing where to begin and how to finish. That's the difference between a trip and a journey. A trip doesn't allow you to exercise self-substance, and a journey forces you to use that substance to find out where to begin and how to finish.

Two Weeks in July

I've never known one person who is so naturally beautiful externally as well as internally. I've learned that what we admire in others is a true reflection of our own goodness, and as my reflection from you stared back at me, I saw what a great man I would become. You're the very essence of a woman. Your beauty, style and grace are the very definition of what it is to be a great woman. Your words of encouragement and your unselfish actions allowed me to believe in myself again, and I am so very honored to say that I came into your presence. Some people go through their whole lives without experiencing what true love, friendship, and spirituality feels like. I've been blessed with that experience with you, and it has instilled a belief in me that one can have it all, if one will accept it all. I marvel at having the opportunity to learn from you and apply that wisdom to my own life; it has been a great accomplishment for my growth as an individual. If your internal beauty could be practiced as a religion, what a wonderful world we would all live in. You are loved, admired, and respected from the very depths of my heart. I eternally salute you.

Lack of Confidence Equals Lack of Vision

When someone lacks confidence, they will also lack vision. Have you ever tried to encourage your better half to get a better job, lose weight or anything that would be productive to their own well-being as well as to the relationship? You may know that your mate is a good person and be baffled about why he or she will not take your encouragement and advice and act on it. The underlying reason is lack of confidence. When people lack confidence they will also lack the vision to achieve better. When you help boost a person's confidence, you will empower that person to achieve personal goals as well as goals that the two of you may have together.

What's the Real Problem?

Most of us have disagreements with our significant others that have nothing to do with the real problem. It is the underlying problem that we must get to and get out. You may have annoyed your partner by doing something little like leaving a door open, but that was not the reason he or she blew up in a rage worthy of a psychiatrist's attention. Our greatest fears about what we feel we can't achieve can sometimes be mistaken for an unwillingness to progress in a positive direction. Sometimes when we try to inspire other people to grow, we run into one of two problems, either the person doesn't have the same vision that we have and therefore our inspiration and support are in vain, or we are inspiring the person to do the physical part but have yet to help them gain the confidence to try it in the first place. Getting to the underlying problem cannot only help you, but it can also saves a lot of headache, time and heartbreak.

There is No Compromise

There is no compromise when it comes to who you really are in a relationship. Don't compromise what you know in your heart is righteous for the sake of lust or because you don't want to have wasted the time that you've already put into the relationship. When you compromise the things that you know are right, you have compromised yourself as a person. Surrendering each and every time is not the same thing as choosing your battles; it can be destructive to your very existence. In life you have to stand for something, or you'll fall for anything.

Raise the Bar

It's okay to raise the bar on the type of individual you would like to date and eventually build something with. If someone is not on the same page as you from the beginning in almost every way, then most likely they will not be there at the end of the chapter. You can't change someone into who you want them to be, so stop trying! It's easier for people to be who they are then to be who they are not! Your loving ways will not rub off on them if they do not aspire to be loving. Your lust may be at an all-time high, and you may have done something in the world you can think of to please the other person, but at some point you will come to understand that an unloving person has to struggle to be loving. A selfish person struggles to be unselfish. When a person has the qualities you need naturally, without struggle, then everything else will not be a challenge.

Why should a man's mind have been thrown into such close,
sad, sensational, inexplicable relations
with such a precarious object as his body?
~Thomas Hardy, 1840–1928

Have a Bad Moment, Not an Entire Bad Day

Life is precious in all its triumphs and difficulties. It is too short to hold onto the nonsense that keeps us from growing. If you have had a relationship that went sour, it's up to you to take that experience and learn from it. Grab the lesson, and let the pain of the disappointment go. Let the "what could have been" go, and move forward, onward and upward. Every second of your life is precious, and no matter what bumps are in the road that lies ahead in this journey we call life, nothing should ever leave you so cold-hearted that you decide you can't continue.

Human beings cling on to their delicious tyrannies and to their exquisite nonsense, till death stares them in the face.
~Sydney Smith, 1771–1845

Chapter 15

Know Your Mate before You Date

I wish that I had taken my mother's advice earlier in my dating life and read the Zodiac signs of potential love interests. The science of the stars can be dead-on about personalities, etc. Why not?? The world's universal language deals with math and science. I now understand that people are much more aligned with their stars than ever thought before. I'm an Aries, and every Aries that I know is so similar to his or her Zodiac traits that it can sometimes be downright scary. I personally don't look at each sign as a deal breaker, but any additional help in the dating field is always appreciated.

ARIES
March 21-April 19

Aries Female

The Aries female is very hard to figure out. She is somewhat of a mystery. She is the actress of her time. She's temperamental and can go form zero to sixty in a matter of seconds when it comes to her emotions. She has the ability and tendency to be domineering and to impose her opinions on those around her. She'll try to push you around, but if you're strong enough to stand up to her, you'll find she's worth the challenge. The Aries woman is usually cheerful and very playful. She is a hopeless romantic and loves the idea of being in love and living happily every after. She's loyal, ardent, sentimental, and earthy. Flattery will get you everywhere with an Aries woman. She loves to be told how beautiful she is as well how good she is in bed. When it comes to crowds and people, the Aries woman loves the spotlight and the attention it brings—can someone say all eyes on her?! The Aries woman will spend like no other; for her, money is meant to be spent She is very optimistic in life and love, but make no mistake—if you cross her in any way you will have hell to pay. When it comes to sex, she will not keep you in the dark about what she wants. She will have sex just about anywhere that suits her. Being firm and gentle is what she wants, but control is what she ultimately likes, and in order to satisfy her thoroughly, you must relinquish control at some point during the course of sex. If she loves the way you handle her overall, you can be sure that she will show her appreciation in all that she does.

Aries Male

The Aries man is a major move maker; he stops at nothing to make things happen. If you show up to a crowded restaurant with a man born under this sign, you can bet everything that you're going to get a table, even if the manager has to create one. He is jealous, and when you're with him you had better not get caught in the arms of another. His generosity is overwhelming when he is in love, but he can also be frugal when he doesn't think your intentions are genuine. When dealing with an Aries man, be sure of what you want because if you don't, anything other than yes is unacceptable. The Aries man is a sucker for flattery especially when it involves sex; tell them he's the best, and you can watch him gloat with pride. His sense of humor is what keeps the party going, and intelligence in a woman is an instant aphrodisiac to him. Most Aries men go for it all when it comes to making money. They love to spend just as much as the Aries woman does, and holding onto money can sometimes be problematic in business. Spontaneity is the key to his sexual drive, and go is the only thing he wants to hear; no foreplay, no teasing, just get right to the action when dealing with a man born under this sign. Please be ready and willing to go in full force.

TAURUS
April 20-May 20

Taurus Female

She is the ultimate seductress, and she exudes sex, which draws men to her all the time, but please understand that what she claims as hers is hers, and no one had better forget that. When she wants something, please get out of her way because she's going to get it no matter what. Phony people had better beware because she will see right through them no matter how many masks they wear to cover up their true intentions. She is very practical when it comes to men. As long as you have something to bring to the table you will find favor in her eyes. The woman born under this sign loves to learn from her mate when she's young and searching for knowledge. If her emotions are in a rattle, she can and will withhold sex until all is clear. If you cheat on a Taurus woman, you can count on her never forgiving you for such betrayal; and a scorned Taurean woman is a bad enemy to have. The Taurean woman appreciates fashion and the finer things in life. The Taurus woman is a demanding lover who loves and invites the drama in the bedroom. Her strong sense of smell can be a turn-on or a turn-off, so always make sure you are in accordance with her sense. Women born under this sign are all woman, so be prepared or don't accept the challenge.

Taurus Male

The most stubborn of all of the zodiac signs, this man knows the value of a dollar and will always surround himself with the finer things in life. From cars to houses, he has to get his money's worth in all that he acquires. When it comes to obstacles, Taurean men love the challenge. They take this aggressiveness to the work arena as well. A man born under the early part of Taurus loves action and can be considered a thrill seeker. When it comes to love, he is only tolerant of people who don't touch his emotions in the wrong way. He is stubborn enough to fight for a losing cause. You can't drive a Taurean; you can only suggest. The Taurus male qualifies as an ideal lover. He is sensitive and understands his partner's feelings. Foreplay for the Taurus male is like planning an attack on a large continent. He studies his potential mate, but his tactics aren't anything out of the ordinary; most would say they're very basic. However, his stamina is what will be appreciated by any lover. Anything outside of the basic you will have to take control of, and he will follow along. Taurus men will never be the life of the party, and they can be very materialistic and love to see what new things you have, but if you bolster your claims of having the finer things in life all respect goes out the door. Taurus men always feel that it's better to show love than to declare it. For men born under this sign, action does speak louder than words.

GEMINI
May 21–June 20

Gemini Female

Women born under this sign can be a hundred women in one. Sympathetic to your problems, she will be the first to give you advice. She continually seeks out different venues for her enthusiasm and energy, but she also is subject to dark moods. When she has no answers to the unknown, that's when her mood can darken and a strong friendship is needed. The Gemini woman is a free spirit and will not be held to one position by anyone. She loves to come and go as she pleases, and the minute someone tries to tie her down, she will bolt like an Olympic track star. She can be friends with anyone easily, but will cut off those she dislikes easily. She finds it hard to stick to one thing because she gets bored very easily; and this can sometimes lead to disorganization in her life. It is very difficult for her to commit to one emotion, which makes her complex in some areas of love and relationships. Women born under this sign can be the life of the party, but they are also subject to self-doubt and dark moods. When this happens, a strong shoulder to lean on always comes in handy. She is constantly changing and rearranging, decorating someone else's home if not her own. Trying new things always grabs her attention especially anything of luxury. In her relations with men she usually plays a poker face until the end while using her sex appeal as a weapon of strategy.

Gemini Male

He is very intelligent and very articulate when speaking. However, if you want this man to be on time to any event, please forget it because he will not be held hostage to the clock. Never try to defeat him in a debate. Words are a weapon that he can wield with devastating effect. His enthusiasm results in his tackling too many tasks at one time; he is the jack of all trades and the master of none. His reaction to failure is not a good one at all. He can be his own worst critic, and this can lead to depression. However, when new and positive energy is thrust upon him, those dark moods are instantly gone. The best jobs for him are jobs that stimulate him and provide a mental challenge. His best role is as a troubleshooter or a business consultant, where the steady stream of new problems will keep him engrossed and he won't have to bother seeing his ideas carried out. Gemini men like to plan the strategy and leave the day-to-day tactics to others. His emotions are often shallow. The future with him is uncertain, but the present is undeniably fun.

CANCER
June 21-July 22

Cancer Female

You need a group of the world's leading scientists as well as the satellites from every country to figure out where you stand with her. Her tenacious memory shocks most men because she can remember snippets of your conversations as if she's been archiving them in a portable manual as you've been conversing. Her affection for anything old-fashioned and elegant can be found in her taste in clothing and furniture. Her desire for security clings to her like a warm winter coat; she must know where her next meal is coming from. She is loyal to friends and to the man she chooses to be her mate. In turn she expects constant affection from her lover. She must be seduced with tender care and affection; don't think this will be a "wham, bam, thank you ma'am." In fact, it will be more likely to develop into an all-or-nothing relationship. When she finds real love and security, she will go all out for her mate. However, if you lose her, she will always be a distant memory. There are two things this woman needs in combination: love and security. She reaches for the kind of love that is more than sex—that means home, children, and a stable relationship. You won't get her into the bedroom until she is sure of your intentions. She may be feminine, but she is no man's fool.

Cancer Male

The Cancer male loves the company of beautiful women, especially if she has a sense of humor and is intelligent. However, when he has won you over he quickly becomes possessive. The woman he loves will have a difficult time living up to his expectations, for he expects far too much. It doesn't help that he tends to sulk and withdraw into his shell when disappointed rather than say openly what is bothering him. The Cancer male looks for a long-term or permanent relationship with a woman. Yet if a rupture does occur, he can move on to a new love because he has the knack of establishing intimacy very quickly. However, anyone who has touched his emotions will never be truly forgotten, no matter what happens later. He is a complex individual whose changing moods make life with him anything but easy and anything but dull. His tenacity of purpose is a good omen for success, and his sensitivity and intellect make him a natural leader in politics, literature, and business.

LEO
July 23-August 22

Leo Female

She is always on display at an important social occasion; she will be the most glittering female ornament. To her, nothing is more important than that men admire and desire her. She not only has to be important to her mate, she has to be his one and only. That limitation, however, does not apply to her. She wants to be free to roam at will and find her prey. Usually she doesn't have to look far. The prey is all too willing. Leo women are the most popular huntresses in the wild. She likes people but is self-centered. She is domineering but dignified, vain but kind. She is a creature of contradictions who sees other people's problems in relation to herself. She is often in love but rarely able to love. She lacks the ability to surrender herself to another persons. She has a great talent for creating her own unhappiness in money matters. She tends to be careless and likes to spend money mainly on herself. A creature who adores luxury, she therefore favors a mate who has the power to keep her in the finer things in life. Other women are envious of her because in a room full of attractive men, she will be the cynosure of masculine attention. She draws men toward her effortlessly. She can be faithful to those who love her, but if their affection falters, that is her license to prowl. In intellectual matters she is daring, resourceful, and adventurous. In her career she does well, although sometime she is difficult to work with because of her insistence that others perform according to her expectations. If a man makes himself important in her life, he can expect to be treated royally.

Leo Male

The Man born under this sign is a magnet for the ladies. Women love him because he is fiery, intense, and masterful. A good friend if need arises, he will take great risk and endure great dangers to guard the safety of those dear to him. He will gamble with life, love and money. He never considers it reckless to go against the odds, for he feels it his destiny to win. He is always falling in and out of love. Romance is not a word to him; it is a way of life. He is only happy when regally wining and dining with a lovely, adorning feminine creature. And sooner or later he will find one whose admiration he cannot do without, and he will marry her. There are not many bachelors under this sign, and alas, their judgment about women is not always the best. Although he expresses a royal contempt for women of loose virtue, he is easily victimized by exactly this type. They know how to play on his central weakness—his vanity. Although he can be creative in business, he tends to sulk. You have to be very careful not to provoke him at such times; however, he does not languish long in depression. There are too many challenges out there waiting to be met and conquer by the King of the jungle. Leo is jealous. Although he dwells on the mountaintop, he is afraid of being dragged down into the valley of competition with lesser mortals. If you have a lover born under this sign, be careful of making him jealous; he can react physically. He is the kind who will beat up a man who flirts with his woman and then beat her up when he gets home. You may find his overwhelming assurance a bit off-putting. But if you are perceptive, you will understand that he is curiously vulnerable.

VIRGO
August 23-September 22

Virgo Female

She can be generous, patient and kind, but she is also a very determined, cool pussycat whose head is always in command of her heart. When she is set on a course of action, her energy is that of a team of women, and she will tackle any task with the conviction that no one can perform it more efficiently than she. Her domain is the home. This is where she rules and a wise man will give her sway. Her dwelling place looks as if no one has ever lived in it. She wants everything in its place and has a place for everything. A wise shopper, she knows how to stretch a dollar until it squeaks. She knows what a man wants. If he can't see it himself, she will help him to analyze the situation. She's very good at analyzing, and she tends to be rather serious and dignified. Modesty is a natural endowment, and you won't find her boasting about her achievements. She has excellent manners, and always conducts herself like a lady—except when provoked for she can unleash a verbal assault like a military machine gun. She worries too much. This is partly because she is convinced that she can reason her way to a solution to almost any problem. Socially she loves small parties, and anything with sophistication attached to it—look out; you've won her over. She doesn't like men who come on too strong with an eye only for sex. It is best for the man to wait until the relationship develops into something, and when it does. look out! She will always be worth the wait.

Virgo Male

The man born under this sign is always interested in anything that will further his career as well as his fortune. The Virgo man is too busy being a perfectionist at his work to bother with romance. He is systematic and careful, and he has a strict sense of responsibility and duty. He is devoted when in a relationship. Fidelity is as important to him as his fortune. However, don't expect an exciting romance; expect security. He has a tight fist when it comes to money; for him a dollar paid is a dollar earned. When he finally marries a woman, it will be after a prolonged courtship, and his choice will be made with careful consideration for the benefit of his future, not just the woman he is involved with. Virgo men are not the type who go around picking up random girls. Usually you can expect that you'll meet him through a mutual friend, etc. He isn't the most exciting date a woman has ever had, bit he will make her feel like she's a princess in his kingdom. In his relationships, he may demonstrate a father figure demeanor. But he's a good bet for the long haul.

LIBRA
September 23-October 22

Libra Female

A woman born under this sign is noted for her beauty. She has an instinct for the finer things in life. She is fastidious in manner and dress, wears subtle, sensuous (and expensive) perfume, loves beautiful jewelry, and tries to surround herself with luxury. She admires beauty in all its manifestations, in music, art architecture and people. She tries to lure any attractive male she meets but will soon move on to a new conquest. She is not uncritical. She expects her image to measure up to high standards and will make whatever corrections are necessary. It's a small wonder that Libra women are considered the epitome of charm. The Libra female tends to prefer the artistic type of man, an actor, singer, writer or musician rather than a boring businessman. Actually, Libra women are not always interested in men, per se. Chiefly, she wants to be admired. She will not be hurried. There is no use in telling her that the dinner invitation is for eight-thirty; by that time she will still be putting on lipstick and applying makeup. After all, any social occasion is nothing more than an opportunity for her to be its shining star. And perhaps she is right, for she is capable of igniting a social evening. She enters a room like a trail of sparkling lights. Her enthusiasm inspires a similar reaction from others. When things don't go her way, she can become petty and carping. She expects perfection and is apt to exaggerate any faults and blemishes that keep her from having it. In her opinion, money is for spending and buying, not for talking about. Talking about money bores the Liberian woman. Her only interest in money is the beautiful things it buys. Don't try to give her orders; she won't obey them. The more pressure you apply, the more she will show you her stubbornness. A kind word and soft persuasion are the only way to break her "won't power." She's a fascinating, many-sided, conscious charmer.

Libra Male

The Libra man was born under the sign of the scales, so balance is an important part of his life. A good conversationalist, he has a strong sense of justice and fair play and will give anyone a fair shake. He has a keen sense of humor and is by nature peaceable and loving. He will resent it keenly when an injustice has been committed. In business he is marvelous, but the Libra man is quite determined to have his way while avoiding the appearance of personal bias or involvement. If things don't go his way, you will suddenly discover beneath his rational, fair, and tolerant exterior a quite different man. He has highly accurate intuitions, so don't try to deceive him. However, if he sees through you, he will try to understand your reasons. And he won't get emotional about it; he hates making a scene. He will be happiest if you display an even temper with not too many emotional highs or lows. He is possessive and what is his better be just that. A woman who knows how to dress is a definite plus. Although Libra men enjoy the finer things in life when it comes to a dollar, you'd better believe that they hold on to it as if it were the last lifeboat on the Titanic. He is not faithful because he doesn't feel deeply; most of his relationships are shallow. He sees nothing wrong with carrying on two or more affairs at one time. There are many ways to annoy Libra males. If they don't really love you, then you'll find yourself by the side of the road with the trash.

SCORPIO
October 23-November 21

Scorpio Female

The Scorpio woman is the most interesting of them all when it comes to passion and persistence. She takes love seriously in the bedroom. She is demanding, and her standards of performance are hard for many men to meet. She has little patience for those who don't measure up or leave her feeling shortchanged. She is stubborn about getting her way. And she has the patience and ability to dissimulate to achieve her goals. All her moves are planned carefully to reach her objectives. It takes a powerful will and real determination to resist her, for she knows what she wants and will press toward it with unremitting force. She cannot be diverted nor will she adapt to changing circumstances. Her intense emotional nature, if frustrated, can become vengeful and destructive. Betrayed, she makes a dangerous enemy. Hell hath no fury like a Scorpio scorned. Jealousy is her worst fault. She expects her lover to reserve all his admiration for her. She finds rivals and intrigues where none are to be found. She treats a lover like royalty, but when her mood changes, and it will, she flays him. Her motto is, "Never go to bed angry." If you have an argument, don't pretend it never happened if you haven't resolved it. She is deeply loyal to the one she loves. If a man meets her halfway she will be his forever. There is no middle road with a Scorpio woman; it can be heaven or hell.

Scorpio Male

The man born under this sign is ruled by passion, emotion and unpredictability. His nature is governed by his desires, and to satisfy them he will accept any challenge and confront any obstacle with no regard for consequences. Let others label him a player; their opinion of him will not inhibit his restless search for sexual adventure. It isn't hard to understand why people are drawn to him like steel filings to a magnet. They respond to his almost hypnotic sensuality. Scorpio never forgets a kindness and never forgives an injury, and if wounded his one aim becomes vengeance. His relations with people usually involve some element of struggle and strife. In any conflict he is an adversary to beware of. He is fierce, headstrong, and tenacious. Those who deal with a Scorpio must be prepared to make extraordinary efforts to maintain the peace. The tender quality of mercy is not his. If you start trouble with him, be prepared to go to the limit because you'll have to. When challenged, Scorpio fights literally to the death. In an argument he will put everything at risk gambling for all or nothing, and let the devil take the loser. His motivations appear complex and mysterious, for he has hidden the private side of his personality. He is dynamic and overbearing but loyal to friends. He does not wish to become dependent but needs someone to lean on. Unstable emotionally, he despises weakness in others. Work is important to him although he dislikes hard physical labor. He has unusual powers of concentration, vivid imagination, great courage and enterprise–attributes that usually spell success. He is also practical in matters of finance. In affairs of the heart, he simply won't take no for an answer. He expects you to commit yourself wholly to him and his needs. If you don't, he will be ruthless about cutting the ties that bind.

SAGITTARIUS
November 22-December 21

Sagittarius Female

The Sagittarius woman is the Don Juana of the zodiac. She is broad-minded in her choice of lovers. A man may attract her because of a particular trait—his enthusiasm, or his ready sense of humor—and she will overlook his other less desirable qualities. She will go from one sexual exploit to another with an easygoing approach so that everyone remains on a friendly basis. However, she is not capable of deep emotional involvement and is more likely to follow the caprice of romantic inclination. She is a gambler at the game of love. Each new lover is a roulette chip she tosses onto what she hopes will be a lucky number. Should an affair go sour, she is philosophical. There'll be another lover along in a little while; why weep for a lost love? She is vain. At the approach of maturity she is likely to take off for the nearest plastic surgeon. The Sagittarian woman wants to entertain and be entertained. She wears her heart on her sleeve, even when she's happy. She can't be happy alone. She needs an audience to witness her happiness. Basically, the woman born under this sign is willing to explore sex with a promising partner, but she is far more interested in friendship, the exchange of ideas, and romantic adventure. She can be a tease, however, and it's sometimes difficult for a man to figure her out whether she's making a sexual overture or just looking for a friend. She is also a good listener, a comrade for a man who likes sports and outdoor adventure, and a marvelous social hostess who enlivens any party and who always attracts to her the most fascinating people. Her impatient, impulsive nature is always at war with her best interests. She would do better in life if she had some understanding of her real strengths and weaknesses. But she's the kind who will always leap twice before she looks and will never accept advice or warning from others. Thin-skinned and easily humiliated, she is a sucker for flattery. A smooth talker can easily win her over. As a result, unscrupulous men often victimize her while Mr. Right gets away. Immature and self-conscious, flighty and changeable, she is hard to understand and nearly impossible to control.

Sagittarius Male

You'll feel more alive the minute you meet him. He's charming, witty, and will convey the impression that you are the most interesting woman he's ever met. Don't be deceived. If you look closely, you'll see that his eyes dance from female to female. The truth is that he wants them all. When a pretty woman enters the room, he will follow her, refreshing her drink offering her party tid-bits, showering her with attention, trying everything in his repertoire to dazzle her. He will get her address and telephone number; besiege her with phone calls, candy, flowers and other gifts. In romance, he is an idealist who thinks that the very next girl will be the one. No matter how many times he's disappointed, his optimism survives. He regards every new day as an opportunity—after all, it's a day he's never seen before. It can be exciting just to wake up and discover it is Tuesday. He has a tendency toward secrecy and will keep a relationship hidden even when it isn't really necessary. Moody and easily depressed, he may also suffer from occasional nervousness and even strange delusions. You may be taken aback by his temper tantrums. He likes to do his own thing and does not willingly make concessions. Experience has taught him that he can get almost anything he sets his ambition to. A woman who marries a Sagittarian should bear in mind that this is a man who, whether married or single, remains, in his heart, a bachelor.

CAPRICORN
December 22-January 19

Capricorn Female

Her gaze is never fixed on the stars. Until she gets over her cautious approach to love, she won't know real fulfillment. To put it another way, when she is too cautious, she ends up having caution itself to be cautious about. Her aloofness will yield as soon as she becomes surer of herself. The truth is that she's afraid of falling in love because she wants to be sure it's the real thing. Basically, she needs to feel secure and protected. Once committed to a lover, she isn't likely to withdraw her affections. She is an all or nothing woman. She is extremely loyal, but she must be loved and wanted in return. That's why she must be aloof and cautious at first; she's trying to size up the possibilities and risks before committing herself. Her emotional guard is up. Unfortunately, she doesn't always know when to let it down. However, the man who really captures her heard and proves worthy of her affections will find an eagerly passionate love partner—a woman who will do anything for her lover. She must be constantly busy to be happy and often becomes involved with charities or causes. She takes life quite seriously and has an inner conviction of her ability to attain high goals. She respects people who are successful and is willing to accept instructions from them. She admires and obeys authority. In the end she will prevail at being the greatest lover, friend or wife you've ever had.

Capricorn Male

He is passionate, strongly sensual, and hates to be refused anything. He won't put up with any coy teasing from a woman. He resents wasting time; however, he will understand if you have well-reasoned objections to leaping into bed with him; he can be patient. An honest statement of how you feel will be enough—if that is how you really feel. Don't try to put on an act. He not only won't like it, he'll see through it. If you give his ego enough encouragement, make clear how much you enjoy his company, he'll be tied to your kite strings for as long as you want him. He's faithful; he doesn't understand why so many men feel the need stray. If you have one good woman, how many do you need? Capricorn is content to be yours alone. He expects you to be a good hostess, a working partner, and a loyal friend. He needs a sense that you two are linked by a romantic destiny. His progress toward a goal is relentless and deliberate as a lava flow. He is a firm believer in singleness of purpose. He knows that all the talent in the world is useless without the ability to work. This is the key to his success in either love or business. A born manager, he will usually climb to the top in whatever field he chooses. He is practical, determined, and ambitious. Those who do him favors along the way will always be rewarded handsomely. He is a sensualist; he seeks the heights of love through sheer physical passion. In an emotional relationship, he demands much and gives as little as possible of himself.

AQUARIUS
January 20-February 18

Aquarius Female

The Aquarius woman is sensitive and possesses a very strong intellect. She lives essentially in her mind. Friends stimulate her. She likes parties and people, excels in socializing, and is always ready to accept a last-minute invitation from someone she likes. Basically honest and open, she is a very poor liar because she doesn't want to be untruthful. When she likes someone, she has a tendency to bare her soul, too often not wisely. What interests her is a challenge. She welcomes any new opportunity and accepts any new responsibility because she feels certain that she will prove equal to whatever is asked of her. Because she is bright, willing to try anything, and understands the motivations of people, she will usually succeed. A true humanitarian, she is very much concerned with problems of the world she lives in. Look for her in the forefront of any battle for social justice, and you'll find her in the underdog's corner. Her native empathy and compassion make her sensitive to the suffering of others. Although she is charming, entertaining and imaginative, she can be stubborn. If she is sure she knows something, she will be very hard to sway, even with hard facts right in front of her. When she makes up her mind, only she can change it. She can be intense, nervous, and when frustrated, somewhat of a nag. Another fault is that she spends too much money and is extravagant about personal comforts. She loves beautiful things, including all parts of the human body. You'd better not forget to compliment her on how great she looks; this woman needs to be appreciated. A natural-born neat freak, nothing turns her off more than a sloppy person. When dealing with an Aquarius woman, please leave your ego at home, and don't forget to bring your cleaning supplies.

Aquarius Male

The first contact has to be made through the mind. He has to respect you as a person before he can be turned on to your charms. Once he is intrigued on an intellectual level, he can be reached on the physical plane. But he cannot attain sexual fulfillment without a previous mind-to-mind contact. Aquarius is definitely not a loner. He is generous, open, and sincerely interested in other people. In fact, he is only happy when involved in the lives of others. He is always searching for an answer, searching for the truth. His nature is analytical. The best way to capture his interest is to present him with a problem. In romance, an Aquarius male responds to the subtle approach and is capable of the most tender emotions. He is highly imaginative—sexually, a frigid a woman won't remain frigid for long with him as a lover. Unfortunately, he often loses himself in dreaming rather than doing. He may fall in love easily, but he hesitates to marry. If you finally get him on the hook, you'll find he's a great catch. He is perceptive, kind, expressive and a good judge of character. Though he may have appeared cool on the surface, he smolders with masculine magnetism. He's basically faithful; if he's occasionally flirtatious, that's because he's so curious about the unknown. Keep a loose reign, and he'll come home again. He can be a lot of fun and very stimulating for the right woman.

PISCES
February 19-March 20

Pisces Female

Ruled by Neptune, the planet of beauty and mystery, she is intensely feminine, sensual, intuitive, and responsive. Her powers of insight make her sympathetic to others. She never stands on the outside looking in. She needs constant reassurance that she is loved. In turn, she will repay a mate with blessings of a truly sensual nature. She has an uncanny knack for getting around people, especially influential, important people. Because she appears both innocent and helpless, she draws forth their protective strength. She falls in love too easily and she dallies with Mr. Wrong when she should be entertaining Mr. Right. Even when happily married, her strong sexual instincts lead her into extramarital affairs. She is not practical and has little understanding of money matters. She sets very high, unrealistic standards for those close to her. Be very aware of her, for she can become vindictive. She has a flair for drama, and you can always count on her to make the right moves, say the right things and create the right ambiance. Pisces would be considered the tease of the zodiac. She will employ all her womanly wiles to capture a new man's interest.

Pisces Male

He is passionate, emotional and unstable. You can expect the unexpected with him. He is constantly pulled by contrary impulses. Unusually sensitive to those around him, he exercises a deep and unconscious magnetic appeal. His nature is warm and responsive, and he sees people not as they are, but as he would like them to be. He is most attracted to a sensuous woman, especially if she has a domineering streak. Constantly lured by change and excitement, he yearns for nothing more than emotional stability. He'll use his superb gifts of creativity but is not too effective in business. One reason is that he much prefers to work alone; another is that he despises hard work and most fields of endeavor. If you want him to do good work; you have to deliberately take the hard way. Pisces' instinct is to find the easy way. He lacks the practical approach, the organizing ability, and the dynamics of the successful executive. The best place for him is on the creative side. He is a procrastinator who simply can't seem to get going. He can act as though he's listening better than most people truly listen.

Chapter 16

Your Zodiac Match

ARIES
March 21-April 19

Aries and Leo

Aggressive Aries finds his equal in Leo who is frank and outgoing sexuality; this relationship is fully a match. Sex is usually straightforward without kinky proclivities. Aries must be sure to flatter Leo on his physical performance. Leo must be sure not to deflate Aries too much and must restrain Aries' inherent tendency to dominate. Otherwise, all systems are a go.

Aries and Virgo

The boldness of Aries is likely to capture the fancy of the reserved Virgo, but their sexual personalities are so dissimilar that a good deal of tolerance is required on both sides. Aries will be charmed by the tact, reticence and control of Virgo. Virgo may not approve of Aries' extravagant ideas about lovemaking and a fear will be intermittent fun but the chances of success in marriage are no better than 50/50.

Aries and Libra

They can develop a short-term affinity for each other. Aries aggressiveness may uncover a streak of unconventionality in Libra. Both love sexual pleasure, but Aries may try to go too far too fast. Libra tends to be idealistic and can be disillusioned. They should practice refinement and the nuances of carnal behavior. A fulfilling physical union will make for a successful affair but not a marriage.

Aries and Scorpio

Sex can be stimulating or frustrating. Those are two ways it can go. Both are biased toward action and blessed with great physical energy, but that they are both independent and aspire to control.

Aries and Aries

Usually what will happen in sexual matters is that the woman will dominate the male. An Aries man won't long be content with the subordinate role. There will be competition as each tries to take the lead, and this causes an increasing number of temperamental fireworks. Eventually this means unresponsive disharmony in the bedroom. Initially a promising affair, a poor prognosis for marriage.

Aries and Taurus

Aries wants to make love on impulse. The cautious deliberativeness of Taurus who rarely does anything on impulse will prove annoying to Aries. If Taurus can allow Aries to lead the way, they can discover new possibilities of physical enjoyment. Otherwise, it's hard to establish a desirable balance. An affair would develop considerable friction and they're really not suited for the long haul.

Aries and Gemini

This union can be exciting because both are restless, active and ready to explore. The tendency of Aries to dominate is curved by Gemini adroitness. Gemini suffers no sexual inhibitions, but its high-spirited energy may seek others for fulfillment. An affair will last for as long as Gemini maneuvers successfully. Marriage may settle Gemini down and prove quite successful.

Aries and Cancer

A powerful sexual attraction is usual between these two signs. The trouble is that when the passions are spent there is little left. Aries doesn't find enough compensation, and they begin to argue over trifles. Temperamental unsuitability leads to further incompatibility in bed. The forecast for an affair is heavy seas and for a marriage it's an almost certain shipwreck.

Aries and Sagittarius

Both are a little bit combative, so there will be plenty of conflict in the sexual arena. Aries' optimism and good humor may overcome Sagittarius' tendency toward moodiness and bring out a playful attitude toward making love. The camaraderie of the bedroom can cast a bivalent aura over the rest of the relationship. A rewarding affair—marriage will be linked closely to the satisfaction of physical desires.

Aries and Capricorn

Aries is forward-looking and eager to experiment. Capricorn is more of a prude. Capricorn passions are more restrained. Aries can upset the Capricorn calculations, awakening the strong libido of its sex partner. If so all auguries are good. Better for marriage than for a short-term affair.

Aries and Aquarius

The physical relationship will be both energetic and innovative. It is probable that Aries will dominate since Aquarius is more passive by nature. Aquarius will not give in and will not accept domination that doesn't seem to be in its best interest. Aries needs tact to deal with this highly emotional dreamer. An unusually eventful affair, and granted mutual understanding, a most rewarding marriage.

Aries and Pisces

Aries will be intrigued by Pisces' almost intuitive boudoir behavior. Aries' vivacious confidence will draw Pisces out of its shy shell. Pisces' sexual fantasies put into practice can be very stimulating. They should have some buoyantly joyful sessions together. Prospects for either an affair or marriage are good if they work out their temperamental differences.

TAURUS
April 20-May 20

Taurus and Taurus

They are not always sexually compatible. The woman tends to be sentimental about love. The male is more inclined to be earthy. An affair can and should be pleasurable, but for marriage, the feelings are mixed.

Taurus and Gemini

Dualistic, variable, changeable, and versatile, Gemini is the opposite of steady, persevering Taurus. Taurus is attracted to the artistic and imaginative side of Gemini. Taurus is likely to intrigue Gemini; however, Gemini will be irritated at the slow Taurus reaction and its plodding amatory. A poor affair and not much better as conjugal partners.

Taurus and Cancer

Taurus finds Cancer a romantic, satisfying partner. Taurus' stability is not shaken by Cancer's moods, and its steadiness of purpose provides firm ground for Cancer's leaning toward procrastination about sex. Both share strong desire for a passionate emotional life. If the physical side is gratifying, this will be a satisfactory affair. Probably a rewarding marriage.

Taurus and Leo

Taurus will have to go along with Leo's grandeur complex. Leo takes as a matter of right its place at the very center of its paramour's life. Leo is vivacious and giving. Taurus tends to be sober and selfish.

There will be little to complain about in the sexual area, but Leo must set the mood and pace. Hard to please Leo may prove troublesome in an affair, and for the long pull, this is not a good combination.

Taurus and Virgo

Taurus is more physical and may be bothered by Virgo's tilt toward the puritanical. In love making, Virgo prefers the simple way and not too much frenzy, if you please. Taurus doesn't mind the simple way but its relentless approach to sex may cause Virgo some disquiet. Otherwise, there won't be too many problems between them. A good affair. A marriage should work but may depend on sexual compromise.

Taurus and Libra

Libra will bring to their sex life a good deal of warmth and the concentration necessary to analyze any physical problems. Libra will make the extra effort to titillate and satisfy. Taurus is also persistent, so the odds are good for mutual fulfillment in this area. Probably a good bet for a more permanent union.

Taurus and Scorpio

They have a considerable sexual appetite in common. Also, neither feels any particular need for outside affairs. If angry, Taurus can be stubborn, and Scorpio's own anger when roused is something of which all signs of the zodiac should be aware. A tempestuous affair is indicated, and marriage is possible only with extreme tolerance.

Taurus and Sagittarius

The danger here is that Taurus will try to tie a string to independent Sagittarius. That can't work. Highly sexed Taurus will be pleased by Sagittarius' lustiness but annoyed by its compulsion to seek love wherever it can be found. They will have fun together but happy-go-lucky Sagittarius is usually a much better lover than mate.

Taurus and Capricorn

Equally strong sexual desires are at work. Neither wants unrestrained, unconventional sex. Taurus won't like Capricorn's native secrecy about what it expects and Capricorn won't like Taurus's attempt to take what it wants. There won't be much romance between these two, but they can have a sensual amour or a very long-term partnership.

Taurus and Aquarius

Introspective Aquarius isn't as interested as Taurus in the physical aspects of love. Aquarius would prefer to commune on a mental plane, but that kind of love won't satisfy passionate Taurus. Aquarius in turn, may feel Taurus is too demanding. A casual affair, an unpromising marriage.

Taurus and Pisces

Pisces has a volatile, unpredictable temperament in a sexual encounter. Taurus may find this hard to handle. By helping Pisces act out his fantasies and by tactful and firm encouragement, a determined Taurus can increase Pisces s receptiveness. The success of the sexual arrangement depends on Taurus. There are good prospects for an ardent affair and for a satisfactory marriage.

GEMINI
May 21-June 20

Gemini and Aries

Both are lively enthusiasts and enjoy variety in their sexual actions. They will not become bored in the bedroom. Aries can give Gemini the firm direction it needs. Aries is stimulated rather than irritated by Gemini's occasional waywardness. An excellent match for a short-term liaison with a good chance to develop into an affectionate long-term alliance.

Gemini and Taurus

Jealous, possessive Taurus can't take flirtatious Gemini. Gemini resents and will try to escape from Taurus's restrictive net. Sexually, Taurus is too dull for Gemini who in turn cannot give Taurus the security it needs. If this sounds like the two signs aren't compatible, you're right. An unhappy short-term affair is the most likely result.

Gemini and Gemini

This might be a lot of fun while it lasts, but it will very quickly become unstable. Except for a transient physical attraction, all signposts indicate the direct route to chaos. Both are flirtatious, compulsive, and easily bored. The course of love will be turbulent and the marriage a probable disaster. In rare instances, this combination does work; however, they are the most interesting couple you will ever know.

Gemini and Cancer

Danger is ahead for this pairing. Cancer is too sensitive and shy to reveal its true feelings. Gemini will play at love while Cancer will take it seriously. Cancer needs praise and reassurance while Gemini can be too crudely frank. These temperamental differences will be a frequent source of trouble in the bedchamber. An affair runs steadily downhill, and marriage will eventually flounder.

Gemini and Leo

Big-hearted, generous Leo will melt in the hands of Gemini and loves it. Gemini is versatile and clever in sexual play. Leo will respond with admiration and affection. Leo is content to let Gemini pursue its own way without carping or suspicion. An ideal mating, their will be excitement and fun in an affair, and chances are also bright for a more permanent relationship.

Gemini and Virgo

A Virgo considers Gemini an immature lover. Gemini considers Virgo a stick-in-the-mud and a bore. Virgo has fixed opinions about sexual conduct. Gemini vacillates after the fires of passion burn low. Virgo will tend to nag and criticize Gemini, and Gemini will turn a roving eye elsewhere in search of variety. A pair of star-crossed lovers who shouldn't count on a long future.

Gemini and Libra

An attractive interesting pairing, both are affectionate and their lovemaking is likely to become fervent. Neither is jealous or possessive, and their temperaments interact to stabilize each other. Both are willing to experiment with sex. They should enjoy an affair and marriage, especially if Libra can convince Gemini to watch the pocketbook. They have an excellent chance for happiness.

Gemini and Scorpio

Sexually compatible, both Gemini and Scorpio prove that raw physical attraction isn't everything. Scorpio is jealous and Gemini is fickle. After a passionate interlude, an affair will quickly cool into unpleasantness and even hostility, and even marriage. Only an exceptional pair will make a go of it.

Gemini and Sagittarius

Both are restless, changeable, and not demonstrative as lovers. Gemini will tend to criticize Sagittarius's performance under the covers. There are other weak points in this relationship, but a source of strength is that neither is demanding or possessive in this relationship. Both have to work at a marriage, but if they do, it can be rewarding.

Gemini and Capricorn

Gemini is too freewheeling and independent for conservative, steady, home-loving Capricorn. Some of Gemini's sexual behavior will prove embarrassing to Capricorn. Capricorn worries about more than its physical needs, (job, money, career) and thinks that Gemini is scatterbrained. An affair is possible, but a successful marriage between these two is proof of love conquering all.

Gemini and Aquarius

Sensitive Gemini understands and appreciates the fantasies of Aquarius. They can become adventurous and inventive lovers. The harm of the relationship will be its unpredictability. The relationship may not always run smoothly, but it will be exciting and rewarding. When the affair is over, they will remain friends. Marriage is likely to be comfortable and pleasant, marked by deep affection rather than passion.

Gemini and Pisces

They will be better at thinking up new sexual schemes than at carrying them out. Pisces are a bit too emotional for Gemini whose impulse is to enjoy the experience and move on. This tends to breed an atmosphere of suspicion and distrust. There can be real affection between these two, but eventually the insecurity will erode the relationship. A somewhat risky affair and an unhappy marriage.

CANCER
June 21-July 22

Cancer and Aries

Aries is somewhat too adventurous a lover for Cancer who tends to be more conventional. Though strong sexual attraction may exist at first, in time Aries may provoke Cancer's moody jealousy, and Cancer will be too easily hurt by Aries' biting tongue. Aries will also find Cancer's possessiveness oppressive. A difficult affair, a marriage headed for the rocks.

Cancer and Taurus

Cancer brings sensitivity and imagination to this union. Both are passionate and don't need outside interests to keep them content. If Taurus is attentive, Cancer will respond in kind. Appreciative of each other's needs, they will both enjoy a successful marriage.

Cancer and Gemini

Cancer's basic insecurity will be aggravated by fickle, flirtatious Gemini. Gemini's unguided sexual energy presents problems to Cancer, causing frustration and difficulties. Cancer will become quite jealous and will try to restrict Gemini's activities, and that only makes Gemini resentful. A highly emotional affair, and a longer relationship that will flounder over basic differences in temperament.

Cancer and Cancer

They are really too much alike to be happy. There is an abundance of sensitivity on both sides which will result in emotional problems.

Both try to lead in sexual encounters, and that provokes frequent criticism and arguments. They are mutually attracted to each other. A marriage will require much sympathy and understanding to survive.

Cancer and Leo

Leo tends to be a stabilizer for Cancer's moods. Leo is also generous with its affections, and that reassures moody, insecure Cancer. On the other hand, Leo requires a great deal of flattery and admiration, particularly for its sexual prowess; it must dominate. If Cancer yields and provides what Leo needs, this could be a passionate affair and a triumphant marriage.

Cancer and Virgo

Virgo's practical, agreeable nature provides a sound basis for this relationship. Cancer is more emotional than reserved Virgo, but they can develop a really warm and affectionate feeling for each other. Sexually they get along quite well, although the heavens don't light with the celestial fires. The problem is that both are shy and retiring and need to make an effort to avoid dullness. A fine affair, and probably a comfortable marriage.

Cancer and Libra

Libra finds it difficult to sympathize with Cancer's brooding temperament. In turn, Cancer becomes insecure and anxious at Libra's detachment. Actually, Libra is rather attracted to Cancer's moods but simply prefers to avoid trouble. If Cancer's affectionate nature is offended, it will lead to difficulties. A possible affair, a risky nature.

Cancer and Scorpio

Scorpio's strength and need to dominate and protect are just what Cancer is looking for. Cancer is more sensitive in sexual relations and Scorpio is more passionate, but Cancer's desire to please helps to avoid any major problems in this area. Love tends to deepen, and a fine affair can grow into a very good marriage.

Cancer and Sagittarius

These two have very opposite goals and different desires Sagittarius is a rover and does not like to be fettered by sexual ties. Cancer needs the security and love that Sagittarius cannot offer. Cancer will be hurt and embittered when Sagittarius becomes bored and begins to look for new prospects. There is a dim future for these two signs.

Cancer and Capricorn

Capricorn can't come up with all the affection Cancer requires, for it has too many other interests. However, there is a strong sexual attraction between these two signs. They will have an interesting bedroom relationship until Capricorn's practicality and reserve begin to look like rebuffs to Cancer. An affair marked by instability and an unpromising marriage.

Cancer and Aquarius

A lone wolf, Aquarius deals too many bruises to Cancer's vulnerable ego. Cancer is more demonstrative and steadfast than adventurous Aquarius. They may get along for a moment in the bedroom, but the partnership will break down in the living room. Cancer's needs may go unsatisfied, as Aquarius tends to absence itself from emotional demands.

Cancer and Pisces

Sexually, this is a good match. Both are highly affectionate, responsive, and provide needed ego bolstering to each other. Cancer will probably take the lead because Pisces tends to be somewhat over-subtle and eccentric in lovemaking. No quells will last long, most will be resolved quickly in bed. A compatible couple who can have great days and nights over the short or long haul.

LEO
July 23-August 22

Leo and Aries

This couple is drawn together, for they share a powerful interest in sex. Both have kind and passionate natures. Aries' compulsion to lead comes up against Leo's desire to rule, and that's like the conflict between the irresistible force and the immovable object. However, the physical rapport is great and should overwhelm problems. A joyful affair, a fine marriage.

Leo and Taurus

Their romantic duet can turn into a vocal tug-of-war. Both are too set in their own ways, and contests of wills can become explosive. They can have an affectionate sexual relationship, but Leo's exuberance will prove annoying to quiet, sedate Taurus. Extravagant Leo will be constantly irked by Taurus's closely watching the buck. A possible affair, but a longer liaison is doubtful.

Leo and Gemini

Gemini has to be clever to keep Leo in thrall, for while Leo is easygoing and tolerant, cuckoldry does not suit its royal image. Gemini's natural instinct to find ways to get along should see them trough. Gemini exasperates Leo. Since Leo is the stronger personality, it will dominate without effort. A fun affair, a fine marriage.

Leo and Cancer

Leo is looking for a more casual affair than Cancer, who wants to become more involved. Cancer wants more than sexual passion; it wants the stamina, the durability, and the little attentions that go with love. Leo may be disposed to give that if it gets all of Cancer's love in return with a little worship thrown in. If not, there will be bad vibes. If so, the stars look down and approve.

Leo and Leo

In the bedroom, as elsewhere, Leo tends to think in terms of first-person singular. Both are romantic and sexually compatible. Each has to let the other shine and share the spotlight if necessary. That isn't always possible, of course, but when it is, long live the King! Long live the Queen!

Leo and Virgo

Leo is more sexually responsive than Virgo, and that can spell trouble in the bedroom. Leo's royal extravagance also causes conservative, prudent Virgo a royal pain somewhere in the anatomy. Virgo doesn't want to be dominated; Leo doesn't want to do anything else. If Virgo starts to criticize, Leo will start to roar. Marriage is a no-go.

Leo and Libra

Leo's approach to sex is more physical and direct than Libra's. However, both will have an entertaining time, for Libra can be quite passionate with the right inducement. Libra must never neglect to pay proper homage to Leo's boudoir mastery and must restrain a proclivity toward too much candor. Leo has to guard its temper. A very good match and probably an enduring one.

Leo and Scorpio

Roman candles, dazzlers, and sparklers in the bedroom. This can do a lot to offset other troubles. Scorpio's jealous anger offends Leo. Scorpio won't offer the respect and admiration Leo needs. Scorpio will try to be possessive, which Leo cannot abide, and each wants to dominate. An affair can be exciting. A marriage should be avoided.

Leo and Sagittarius

Both signs have a keen sense of love as an adventure. They are extroverted, passionate, and pursue their own sexual inclinations without awakening resentment in the other. Both desire frequent intercourse. Sagittarius stimulates and inspires Leo, and Leo evokes from Sagittarius whatever loyalty Leo is capable of. An affair is great fun, and a happy marriage is guaranteed.

Leo and Capricorn

Capricorn's practical approach puts a halter on Leo's expansive, optimistic personality. There are fundamental differences between them. Leo's glamour will be dimmed and even diminished in this relationship. Capricorn is not as romantic or affectionate as Leo and can be too demanding. Leo's extravagance will be annoying to Capricorn. A shack-up may be pleasant, a marriage probably not.

Leo and Aquarius

Aquarius sparks Leo's sexual individuality and lends excitement to their lovemaking. While Leo is intrigued, it is also angered by Aquarius's tendency to analyze and expose. That shakes Leo's confidence in its sovereign powers. Also, the emphasis on unworthiness in the bedroom will get on Leo's nerves. Transient sex partners, impossible marital partners.

Leo and Pisces

Both are more prone to receive than to give. An initial magnetic attraction builds toward an eventual explosion. Pisces is the weaker sign, and its lack of ambition disturbs Leo. When Pisces sulks, Leo's pride prohibits showing sympathy. A difficult affair, a most unhappy marriage.

VIRGO
August 23-September 22

Virgo and Aries

Virgo may be intrigued by audacious Aries. But Aries needs a passionate bedmate, and Virgo is too inhibited to fill the bill. Aries is always looking for an adventure. Virgo likes stimulating talk; Aries like stimulating action. An unlikely affair, and a marriage certainly not made in heaven.

Virgo and Taurus

Taurus likes to enjoy its sex without too much fuss, while Virgo likes to analyze, examine, and perhaps criticize. Otherwise, Virgo proves a willing if not passionate partner for Taurus. In other areas there is true compatibility. Both are materialistic, practical, admire efficiency, and are homebodies. A happy, though not too exciting, affair and a decidedly workable marriage.

Virgo and Cancer

Virgo provides the emotional security that Cancer needs and the little attentions that prove affection. Cancer's dependence finds its perfect answer in Virgo's need to be protective. Cancer's imagination is stimulating to Virgo, and Cancer's eagerness to please deepens Virgo's affection. Both will come out of their shells and begin to enjoy life. An ardent affair, a lasting marriage.

Virgo and Leo

Leo is highly sexed, and Virgo is more interested in security than a roll in the bed. There will be arguments about this and about Virgo's tendency to criticize because Leo is and must remain above criticism. Virgo's practical, down to-earth approach also conflicts with Leo's expansive optimistic nature. An affair is probably a one-night stand; a marriage is a disaster.

Virgo and Virgo

They share a sexual reserve and consider a love relationship the basis for something more important—a life partnership. Demands in the bedroom will not be excessive, but that doesn't rule out complaint and criticism about what does and does not take place. Virgo simply can't help it. A tense affair, but marriage is good if boredom doesn't set in too early.

Virgo and Libra

Loving and affectionate, Libra is rebuffed by Virgo's cool and analytical manner. Virgo is overcritical and undermines Libra's self-confidence. The signs have little in common. An affair is difficult, and it's better not to even think about marriage.

Virgo and Scorpio

These two are basically compatible, although Virgo tends to chill Scorpio's sexual ardor. Scorpio keeps trying to make Virgo wake up to more sensual enjoyment, and Virgo wonders why Scorpio is so aggressive—can't they be friends as much as lovers? If Virgo is willing to compromise, Scorpio stays tractable. An interesting affair with good vibes for a permanent relationship.

Virgo and Sagittarius

Sagittarius's happy-go-lucky approach to love can drive Virgo crazy. Virgo's sense of security really suffers in this relationship. Virgo's prudish attitude toward sex is a major turn-off for Sagittarius, which prompts Sagittarius to look for other sexual outlets. The two might make it for a weekend together, but not for life.

Virgo and Capricorn

Virgo is sexually drawn toward Capricorn, but the fireworks may fizzle. Virgo will find itself taking second place to Capricorn's extra boudoir interests, and this may cause a certain conflict. Otherwise, the two signs work very well together. Both are practical, emotionally reserved, thrifty, and intellectually active. An affair could be rather dull; a marriage will be strong and good.

Virgo and Aquarius

Both tend to think of romance more as an intellectual pastime than a physical exercise. This ideal relationship is marred by the intrusion of other practical differences. Virgo is straight-laced about sex, and Aquarius veers toward the erratic. Virgo thinks Aquarius neglectful; Aquarius thinks Virgo unresponsive. Love will tend to diminish rather than grow with time. A realistic affair, an unwise marriage.

Virgo and Pisces

For Virgo, love is closely allied with security, physical needs with mental compatibility. For Pisces, love is all-encompassing, the central charm of life, beauty and romance and emotional excitement. Virgo's careful, disciplined approach to sex goes all awry when it comes up against the grandiose, unrestricted desires of Pisces. Unless Virgo can break the reserved approach to sex, this union is headed for disaster.

LIBRA
September 23-October 22

Libra and Aries

This relationship suffers from an underlying tension. Aries is aggressive and restless while Libra seeks perfection and needs peaceful companions. This basic disparity of temperament leads to inevitable quarrels. However, the sexual relationship should be good. Fine bedroom, poor living room is the prognosis that adds up to a likely affair and a quite unhappy marriage.

Libra and Taurus

Taurus is too possessive and earthy for romantic Libra. Libra may soon have a very jealous mate on its hands. However, they are physically in tune, and that helps. Libra is considerate and understanding and will cope with Taurus's temper and stubbornness. A tendency toward fickleness in Libra might drive Taurus wild. Fun and games, but longer odds against a durable union.

Libra and Gemini

Both find it difficult to restrict their affections. Love can make the world go round, but this pair gives it a shove. Except for this one problem, however, theirs is an ideal mating. Both are passionate; neither is particularly jealous or possessive. They share many personality traits and are great company in bed. A fine affair, and a warm and happy marriage.

Libra and Cancer

Cancer can be overcritical, especially about Libra's extravagance. Cancer likes to stay close to home, and Libra likes to wander. Not much compatibility here. Deeply affectionate and trusting Cancer will be shocked by Libra's shallow emotions and inconsistency. A tolerable affair, and an intolerable marriage.

Libra and Leo

These two supply each other's wants and needs. Leo is passionate and demonstrative; both are hooked on sex. It will be shooting stars all the way in the bedroom; if egos clash, Libra must yield, however. That won't be too difficult because Libra is usually cooperative. Strategy and tact are Libra's weapons. A torrid affair can become a pretty warm marriage, too.

Libra and Virgo

Virgo lives by the rule book, and that is not Libra's way. And there are other personality pitfalls. Virgo is a penny-pinchers; Libra finds this unforgivable. Virgo can also be nagging and critical, even dictatorial. Libra will resent this and start looking elsewhere for appreciation. A dubious affair, a most difficult marriage.

Libra and Libra

They respond to each other with equal passion. They have much in common; they are socially affectionate and love harmony and beauty. But when the first kiss is over, hard reality intrudes. Neither one wants to come down off of cloud nine. Their lovemaking may take on ho-hum overtones. An affair should work; a marriage requires more maturity and more practical attitudes.

Libra and Scorpio

Scorpio is too jealous for easy-going Libra. Scorpio's renowned jealousy won't put up with minor flirtations. Libra's casual manner toward sex keeps Scorpio seething. Scorpio must dominate. Libra must cooperate. There is a good deal of physical magnetism, but a magnetic field can build to an explosion. A passionate stormy affair or marriage.

Libra and Sagittarius

Sagittarius has a strong penchant for adventure and will never bore Libra. Both are sexually well-mated. The problem lies in Sagittarius's reluctance to settle down and need for independence. Libra wants a real partnership and a pleasant home base. If they can work out these differences, a short or long-term relationship will prevail.

Libra and Capricorn

Capricorn has a strong physical attraction toward Libra who finds Capricorn's knack for making money useful, but Libra's lazy ways offend Capricorn's nose-to-the-grindstone attitude, and Libra is frustrated by Capricorn's sober practicality. Capricorn won't like Libra's socializing. There are too many personality conflicts here for a successful marriage; an affair will be short-lived.

Libra and Aquarius

These two should get along famously. Libra looks to Aquarius for leadership and adventurous living. They enjoy socializing and will become involved in public affairs. They have many friends but also feel free to pursue their own special interests. And they will make love beautifully even if they forget to make the bed. A sexy affair, and a stimulating marriage.

Libra and Pisces

A complicated combination. Pisces's gentleness, sensitivity and emotion are what Libra likes. However, Pisces is not a dominant sign, and Libra is unwilling to supply the firm leadership required. Libra begins to resent Pisces's clawing dependency, and Pisces disapproves of Libra's other interests. When Libra turns into a scold or nitpicker, Pisces wallows in misery. Sad, yes for any marriage or serious affair.

SCORPIO
October 23-November 21

Scorpio and Aries

A highly volatile combination. In sex, Aries is innovative and Scorpio provides enthusiastic cooperation. But Aries is too happy-go-lucky for jealous Scorpio. Both are self-centered, dynamic, and ambitious. The attraction between them may be strong, but individualism tends to pull them apart. Indications point to a short affair, a rocky long-term relationship.

Scorpio and Taurus

Both have the stamina and passion to satisfy each other in bed. But their personality differences will have to be ironed out if they're to keep liking each other in the morning. Scorpio scorns laziness and is basically thrifty. Taurus is indolent and likes to spend the money it earns. Both are proud, stubborn, and domineering. Their strong sexual urges indicate a possible affair. Marriage is extremely dubious.

Scorpio and Gemini

Sexually they get along, but that's not the whole story. Concessions on both sides are necessary. Gemini takes everything too lightly for intense Scorpio. Scorpio is determined, while Gemini is changeable and shifting. Gemini is intellectually keen and enjoys showing off on any social occasion; Scorpio considers that a hideous waste of time. A fluctuating affair, a difficult marriage.

Scorpio and Cancer

These two water signs should get along very well. The sexual prognosis is also good: Scorpio's passion finds a willing partner in Cancer. Physical compatibility helps to reduce the jealous traits from which both signs suffer. Good affair, fine marriage.

Scorpio and Leo

Both signs are on a short fuse, and the explosive disagreements might end in violence. Passion runs high here. They are physically attracted to each other, but Scorpio cannot give the attention and respect that Leo needs. Leo's pride will be hurt, and in many situations Scorpio's jealous possessiveness will be wounded. Perhaps an exciting liaison, but a horrible marriage.

Scorpio and Virgo

Their interests are similar in many areas, but the sexual sphere is not one of them. This makes it hard for them to work out a relationship. Virgo may turn to carping, and a Scorpio will be brutally frank. If Virgo can make the necessary adjustments, it might work. A meeting of minds for a while, but Scorpio will soon start looking for other sexual outlets.

Scorpio and Libra

Scorpio is too possessive for Libra; Libra is too lazy and too sensitive for Scorpio. However, they are both passionate (although Libra is on again and off again). And they will take seriously the responsibility of living together. There will be a problem about Libra's love of luxury, which Scorpio may not be able supply. Stormy weather during an affair. Marriage won't be smooth sailing either.

Scorpio and Scorpio

Sexually these two could start a fire underwater. But they are too much alike. Both are determined, possessive, and jealous, and they have terrible tempers. When they differ, the crockery will start to fly, and the relationship will fly out the window. Their initial intense attraction can't survive outside the heated environs of the bedroom. A great affair but a horrible marriage.

Scorpio and Sagittarius

Don't bring an expensive house warming gift to these two. Scorpio loves its home but Sagittarius has a bag packed and ready to go. Sagittarius must have freedom; Scorpio is overly possessive and demanding. Not even the Sagittarian sense of humor can bridge the chasm that will open between them. Their only attraction is sex, and that won't last. For a night, yes for a lifetime, no.

Scorpio and Capricorn

Both are willing, ambitious, and get along well sexually. There should be a minimum of problems. Scorpio tends to be more emotional, which is good for Capricorn's brooding and inward nature. Capricorn welcomes the security that is implied in Scorpio's possessiveness. Scorpio doesn't mind sex without sentiment, and that suits Capricorn, too. A warm affair, a strong marriage.

Scorpio and Aquarius

Aquarius is involved in many projects outside the home, which is where Scorpio's interest lies. Scorpio can't dominate Aquarius, which prizes its liberty too much. Aquarius is very social; Scorpio is not at all. Scorpio has no use for Aquarius's impractical scheming. This couple should just go their separate ways.

Scorpio and Pisces

This couple has strong fascination for each other. Pisces will depend on Scorpio's strength to bolster its indecisiveness and will positively revel in Scorpio's possessiveness and dominance. Their sex life should be exciting—Pisces is imaginative, Scorpio is preserving. For either an affair or a marriage, you should have it so good.

SAGITTARIUS
November 22-December 21

Sagittarius and Aries

Although they are highly compatible, their mutually combustible natures guarantee plenty of fireworks. However, arguments are short-lived. They get a kick out of doing things together in and out of the bedroom, and they will have lots of friends. Both enjoy an active recreational and sports life. If sex is good, everything else should be great. That includes either an affair or marriage.

Sagittarius and Taurus

Taurus wants to dominate, and Sagittarius won't be dominated. In sex, it's probable that Taurus's steady passions will not be requited by Sagittarius's occasional impulsive desires. Taurus's practical, home-loving nature will also be offended by Sagittarius's restless seeking for adventure. Self-discipline is needed for even a short stay: a minor miracle is needed for a long one.

Sagittarius and Gemini

They are far too restless and rootless for any true compatibility. They quickly develop other interests and drift off to follow them. Both are fun-loving and enjoy each other's company for a time, but Gemini will turn critical and Sagittarius will be driven via the short route to distraction. Nearly hopeless, but on rare occasions it can be exciting.

Sagittarius and Cancer

These two are at the opposite ends of the zodiac. Cancer needs security and stability while Sagittarius wants to be free to venture. Cancer is too sensitive to put up with outspoken Sagittarius. There might be a workable sexual harmony, but Sagittarius soon feels the iron bars of being caged in and soon wants s to fly away. They will be better friends than lovers.

Sagittarius and Leo

This relationship offers great openness and freedom. Leo holds the passion key that can unlock Sagittarius. They should be exciting bed companions. Both also respect each other and enjoy each other's company. They share a love for adventure and cope with hard times with optimism. This is a marriage made in heaven.

Sagittarius and Virgo

Their relationship will deteriorate. Sagittarius's happy-go-lucky approach drives Virgo crazy. Sexually they strike occasional sparks but that still leaves 23 hours out of the day. Virgo is inclined to take the road to the simple life, which is in total contradiction to the wild and impulsive ways of Sagittarius. This relationship is a no-go from the gate!!

Sagittarius and Libra

Libra's tolerance is just what Sagittarius needs. Both are sexually responsive, and considerate Libra will bring out the best in this partner. They will enjoy each other, find little reason to quarrel, and will have many friends and outside-the-home interests. Good vibes here both for the short and long term.

Sagittarius and Scorpio

Sagittarius thwarts Scorpio's passionate nature. Trouble lurks if Sagittarius follows a natural inclination toward freedom and independence, for Scorpio's need is for a loyal mate who can be depended on. Sagittarius has a quick temper that soon cools. Physically they may be compatible for a time, but marriage won't be a many-splendored thing.

Sagittarius and Sagittarius

The general unpredictability of their lifestyles makes a combination that brings out the worst in both. Their restless, independent natures will sooner or later seek freedom—from each other. They are ships that pass in the night; they won't make port together on a long voyage.

Sagittarius and Capricorn

Sagittarius and Capricorn's cautious, plotting nature is appalled by the impulsive carelessness of Sagittarius. Capricorn's demands prove irk-some, and Sagittarius' frank, outspoken reaction offends Capricorn. Money also presents a problem. Capricorn is thrifty, and Sagittarius' frank, outspoken reaction offends Capricorn. Sagittarius is a free spender who wants everything money can buy. A rising tide of discontent swamps these two.

Sagittarius and Aquarius

They share a love for adventure and for getting involved in outside affairs. Sex will be innovative, whether in the bedroom or outside on the roof of the car. Nether is jealous, and neither will try to dominate the other. They will be a fun-loving couple whose love will only deepen in marriage.

Sagittarius and Pisces

Neither provides the reliability that the other requires. There are moments of passion, but the sword of Damocles hangs on a frayed thread over this couple. Sagittarius feels hemmed in by Pisces' timidity, and its energy and optimism slowly sink into a swamp of depression. A most difficult romance, and a virtually impossible marriage.

CAPRICORN
December 22-January 19

Capricorn and Aries

Both are strong-willed, aggressive and won't be bossed. If you think that's a set-up for combat rather than romance, you're probably right. While they may be compatible in bed, there will be arguments about money, friends, who will make decisions, and careers. Throw in a little jealousy just to keep the cauldron bubbling. An affair might work. Marriage is much less promising.

Capricorn and Taurus

Both value security and money as the important foundation to sustain a life of peace. Taurus has patience, and Capricorn is willing to work toward a common goal of mutual enjoyment. Sexually these two are a match made in heaven and their dreams of whatever in the bedroom could come true. Fine marriage and romance.

Capricorn and Gemini

Distinctly different sexual personalities. Gemini is impulsive, flirtatious, and excitable. Capricorn is slow, faithful, and cautious. Any initial attraction is the fabled one of opposites and can't endure. Ambitious, materialistic Capricorn will not long tolerate Gemini's capricious, indecisive ways. Love can't conquer all.

Capricorn and Cancer

Cancer is a little shy sexually, but Capricorn is willing to take the lead. More demonstrativeness from both would help in the preliminaries.

GIVING LOVE A CHANCE / 149

Any rapport they establish in the bedroom will be sorely needed to see them past other obstacles. They are zodiac opposites with all that implies. Capricorn will become too demanding and domineering for sensitive Cancer. An affair is just a matter of time.

Capricorn and Leo

Leo thinks Capricorn is stingy with affection, doling it out like pennies. Capricorn is too unimaginative a partner for Leo, who likes more fire between the sheets. They don't suit each other well physically, and they are both independent and dominant signs who try to rule outside the bedroom. In an affair these differences may be ignored; in a marriage it just isn't likely.

Capricorn and Virgo

Capricorn's practicality and Virgo's neatness go very well together. Sexual fire may turn into a smoldering smoke signal soon after the affair begins, but other traits work together so harmoniously that perhaps these two won't care. Both are dependable, conservative, understanding, and with this in line, a marriage will have a great forecast even if the sexual energy is dull.

Capricorn and Libra

Libra's charm and sexual magnetism attract Capricorn at first, but when the bloom is off the rose, Capricorn finds Libra too self-centered and unresponsive to its physical needs. Marriage won't work unless there is financial gain in the alliance to satisfy Capricorn.

Capricorn and Scorpio

Sex between these two is gratifying. Scorpio is more imaginative and Capricorn more methodical, but they are quite compatible in this area, and success in the bedroom opens up other areas of affection. Both are strong-willed, but Scorpio tends to dominate. Capricorn understands that Scorpio's possessiveness is really a symptom of love. A passionate affair, and a successful marriage.

Capricorn and Sagittarius

These two will never work out, and if they do it will take a miracle to keep them together. Sagittarius's irresponsible spending habits are contrary to more conservative Capricorn who worries about security and the future. Sagittarius's take-a-chance attitude will frustrate Capricorn, which will lead each to go their separate ways.

Capricorn and Aquarius

Aquarius can't stay in love with staid, practical Capricorn. A tolerable affair; a marriage really requires work. Aquarius is a little too much for Capricorn to handle. Freedom loving Aquarius can't handle the stay-at-home, conventional ways of Capricorn, so this relationship will require that both parties give it the best they can at all times.

Capricorn and Pisces

Pisces will try to con Capricorn because that's just the way Pisces is, but Capricorn can handle that and will take control in bed. Pisces is soon to follow. Pisces is also loving and sincere enough to keep Capricorn happy and secure. These very different people supply each other's emotional needs. Good for each other and a lasting affair.

Capricorn and Capricorn

Their romantic life quickly settles into a rut. It can only be successful if both are willing to accept less than they originally hoped for. Neither will experiment or in any way try to enlarge their horizons. The bedroom becomes a suburb of Dullsville. On the other hand, both work hard, are frugal, and serious-minded. An affair or marriage may not be much fun, but they might satisfy each other.

AQUARIUS
January 20-February 18

Aquarius and Aries

There's going to be fun and frolic in the bedroom. Difficulty may arise if either tries to force the other to do anything, for neither can tolerate a domineering partner. They are both imaginative in sex and compatible in other areas. Forceful Aries will take the lead. Chances are excellent either for an affair or a more lasting relationship.

Aquarius and Taurus

Passionate, highly sexed Taurus finds Aquarius's offhand attitude toward sex baffling. Aquarius is also too involved with outside activities to suit home-loving Taurus. There will be frequent personality clashes between two strong-willed people who can't compromise. Bad vibes for the long term.

Aquarius and Gemini

Aquarius is likely to dominate Gemini who goes along with its sexual preferences. There will be a great deal of gaiety in the bedroom and little feeling of pressure or passion. If Gemini becomes interested in Aquarius's outside activities, they will have an interesting affair and a fascinating marriage.

Aquarius and Cancer

Emotional Cancer annoys Aquarius by making sex too important. Aquarius prefers cooler passions and a more casual attitude. In time, Aquarius will feel hemmed in and begin to resent clinging Cancer.

Rebuffed, Cancer will grow surly and feel unwanted. An affair has many difficulties. A marriage has very serious problems.

Aquarius and Leo

This can become one big mess. Although for a time it may seem like hope is alive, the two will come to a crossroads where Leo will want to rule on all matters, especially when it comes to sex. Aquarius's analytical approach toward the bedroom action will frustrate and annoy Leo. A marriage will never be a happy union because of the lack of attention Aquarius will give to Leo's need for praise.

Aquarius and Virgo

Neither excitement nor initiative is to be found here, for both need more erotic stimulation. Sober, practical Virgo also tends to be critical of expansive, generous Aquarius. A quiet affair will wind down to ennui. A marriage just might survive on common interests outside the bedroom.

Aquarius and Libra

Both are warm, sensitive, sexual creatures. Libra's leaning toward erotic games is just what's needed to win Aquarius's wholehearted participation. Each fulfills the other's physical requirements quite satisfactorily. They share other interests also; they both like luxury, enjoy art and music, and freely spend money. An exciting affair, an unusually happy marriage.

Aquarius and Scorpio

Scorpio is so jealous and possessive that Aquarius simply can't put up with it. Aquarius is so indifferent to sex that Scorpio's aggression toward sex will turn Aquarius completely off, for there has to be something outside the bedroom to stimulate Aquarius. An affair will be short-lived.

Aquarius and Sagittarius

Both are social, like to be away from the home, and are interesting, vibrant people who won't be jealous of each other's private lives. They are excellent partners for a short- or long-term arrangement. Sagittarius's wide range of interesting sexual fantasies is a mental turn-on for Aquarius.

Aquarius and Capricorn

They are both undemonstrative lovers, and the combination is likely to be a washout sexually. Capricorn enters physical relationships with caution, and Aquarius isn't likely to be turned on by that approach. Aquarius can't understand provincial, practical, possessive Capricorn. An affair may begin but will go nowhere.

Aquarius and Aquarius

Admirably suited, both are inventive lovers and stimulate each other mentally and physically before, during, and after intercourse. They are right on target sexually. However, there is no deep emotional involvement. Both are too rational, sensible, and moderate. They have many interests outside of each other. A pleasant affair, a sound marriage.

Aquarius and Pisces

Sexual intimacy between these two soon develops into an emotional tug-of-war with hurt feelings and soap opera misunderstandings. Sensitive Pisces is quite dependent on Aquarius and demands constant proof of love. Aquarius feels hampered and hindered by the tentacles of its clinging vine. They are at cross-purposes often. An affair may start promisingly but won't go the route.

PISCES
February 19-March 20

Pisces and Aries

Dynamic Aries unlocks Pisces's full potential in the bedroom. Aries, of course, dominates, but this is what Pisces is looking for. However, tact is necessary for the combination to work in other areas. Pisces is very sensitive to criticism, and Aries is frequently blunt. If they work out their differences, this can be a sexy, enduring relationship.

Pisces and Taurus

They are almost equally passionate, but highly sensitive Pisces needs the special kind of consideration not often forthcoming from down-to-earth Taurus. Far more emotional and sentimental, Pisces is likely to suffer from hurt feelings if taken too matter-of-factly. If this problem can be overcome, there's a good chance this combination will work. A sensual affair, a satisfactory marriage.

Pisces and Gemini

Two unstable signs make an un-promising sexual combination. There may be physical attraction, but Gemini is too changeable and Pisces too sensitive for it to last. Gemini's thoughtlessness will offend Pisces. Both are so egocentric that there will be little attempt made at an accommodation. They need stronger, more dominate partners. A short, possibly heated affair; a quite infelicitous marriage.

Pisces and Cancer

Cancer is likely to prove a demanding lover, but Pisces won't object to that. Both are sexually demonstrative and may spend a good deal of time in the bedroom. Cancer takes the lead and makes the most decisions. Despite some quarrels, on the whole they satisfy each other's emotional needs and are careful of each other's sensitivity. A highly compatible couple.

Pisces and Leo

Fire and water do not mix. Introspective Pisces, even in the bedroom, frustrates outgoing Leo. Neither quite understands the other. Sentimental Pisces begins to pull on Leo and drives it to seek satisfaction elsewhere. Pisces languishes at home dreaming its sad dreams while Leo roams abroad. An affair will be difficult, marriage will be unrewarding.

Pisces and Virgo

Overly affectionate Pisces does not get much satisfaction from reserved Virgo. Virgo resists Pisces's excessive sexual demands and turns hypercritical and faultfinding. There are other problems, too. Practical, logical Virgo won't indulge Pisces's extravagant tastes or put up with emotional waywardness. Virgo will make plans while Pisces acts on the spur of the moment—then changes its mind. A quarrelsome affair, a joyless marriage.

Pisces and Libra

They have difficulty relating to each other except in a physical way. If they hit it off there, chances are still dim that it will develop into anything worthwhile. Libra won't supply the kind of dominance that

Pisces needs. Both like luxury, but neither is willing to work hard to achieve it. A disjointed affair, a marriage that eventually turns bitter.

Pisces and Scorpio

They should enjoy a deep and satisfying physical union. Excellently matched as lovers, Scorpio's strength provides the firm support that Pisces needs in other areas. Pisces will not provoke Scorpio's jealousy and construes Scorpio's possessiveness as a form of love—which it is. Both quickly ignite as lovers and find complete gratification. The sooner these two take the vows the happier they'll be.

Pisces and Sagittarius

They may have their moments erotically speaking, but Sagittarius is independent and venturesome, and Pisces, sensing this, becomes ever more dependent and emotionally clutching. Pisces's languorous lovemaking is simply a bore to restless Sagittarius, who wants to move on to other interests. Sagittarius will be tempted to provoke and mock Pisces's sentimental yearnings. An affair will end almost as soon as it begins; marriage would be disastrous.

Pisces and Capricorn

A fine sexual pairing. There may be minor problems and misunderstandings, but these two are well-equipped to work through to a solution. Strong, dominant Capricorn knows how to make Pisces feel desirable and secure. Pisces, in turn brings a breath of romance into solid Capricorn's emotional life. Their differences complement each other and assure a very good affair or marriage.

Pisces and Aquarius

Sexually they may find each other stimulating for a time, for both are imaginative lovers. But self centered, subjective Pisces has little in common with outward-directed, social Aquarius. Independent and determined Aquarius won't spend the precious effort to bolster and reassure Pisces. Aquarius tries to solve problems with logic, Pisces with emotion. This will defeat them in the long run.

Pisces and Pisces

Mutual empathy provides a wonderful understanding of each other's sexual needs. If their problems could be absorbed by sheer physical compatibility, this would be one of the zodiac's best matches. However, these emotional leeches spoon drain each other's reserves. Without a strong, dominant partner, they go off in wrong the directions. A highly sensual affair, but marriage will end in increasing sexual indulgence and possible depravity.

Sixx King
Producer/Director/Actor/Activist

Sixx King is one of today's most promising writers/producers/directors/actors/activists. A natural organizer, mobilizer and pop culture maven, King is always on the cutting-edge of what's new and hot in entertainment. Through his company, New Wall Street Media, King has produced music videos for some of the industry's brightest artists.

In 2003 King shocked the live television audience by his bold stance at The Grammys. This spawned his hilarious and infamous DVD, Crashing Hollywood. A once in a life time interview on Howard Stern paved the way for King's radio career with New York's Hot 97 morning show. During that same year he appeared in his fourth feature film, Black Cloud starring Tim McGraw and Rick Schroder.

In 2008, King was tapped as an on air personality for Radio One WPHI 100.3 The Beat and WRNB 107.9, taking home the March Of Dimes A.I.R. award for Best New On Air Talent. Also in 2008, King formed Youth, Politics'& Empowerment, a program that introduces young people to film and television producing while learning about the political process.

While recovering from a few failed relationships, King began blogging about these topics which lead him to the prestigious Essence magazine online audience. His open candor was an immediate hit with the all female magazine audiences and inspired his first book entitled, Giving Love A Chance The Secrets to Men Women and Relationships.

The highlight of King's career is his commitment to his son and the community. As a father King believes that what children become today is what our future will become tomorrow.

GIVING LOVE A CHANCE